Academic
Listening Strategies
A Guide to Understanding Lectures

Julia Salehzadeh
The University of Michigan

Michigan Series in English for Academic & Professional Purposes
Series Editors: John M. Swales & Christine B. Feak

ANN ARBOR
THE UNIVERSITY OF MICHIGAN PRESS

This book is dedicated to my parents,
Ruth and Tom Risch,
who believed in me before I could.

Published in the United States of America
The University of Michigan Press

Manufactured in the United States of America

Printed on acid-free paper

2009   2008   2007   2006   4   3   2   1

Acknowledgments

I am extremely grateful to many individuals who made significant contributions to these materials. I would like to thank John Swales whose influence has seeped into these pages as well as the video clips. He gave thoughtful advice from the earliest drafts of this text, allowed himself to be videotaped on numerous occasions while we experimented with equipment and content, and provided gentle encouragement to keep at it.

I would also like to thank David Erdody for providing technical know-how and for his patience while videotaping and experimenting with various formats for the video clips. Thanks, David, for pursuing excellence with me and for enabling me to put the listening material into the students' hands.

I'd like to thank all of the professors and other lecturers at the University of Michigan who graciously allowed us to videotape them on several occasions and then allowed us to dissect their lectures. Thank you to Professors Keith Alpine, Alan Deardorff, Harold Pollack, Marilynn Rosenthal, and Herb Winful. Thank you Ricardo Carvajal and Officer Mathews.

I would also like to thank my colleagues Christine Feak, Joan Morley, Susan Reinhart, and Lise Bucholtz for their valuable comments on drafts of this text.

Thank you to Elie Mosseri for expert technical editing asssistance. I am also grateful to my students who have endured various permutations of these materials and the technical glitches inherent in this experimental endeavor. Thank you Kong, Nam, and Xiaoyu for your contributions.

Thank you to Nick Ellis, Elizabeth Axelson, John McLaughlin, Christine Feak, and Lindsay Crammond for permitting us to use your photos. Thank you to all the people who created the Michigan Corpus of Academic Spoken English (MICASE) database and made it user-friendly, and thanks to Sara Pilar for her data on contractions. Thank you to Rita Simpson for granting permission to use material from the MICASE, R.C. Simpson, S.L. Briggs, J. Ovens, and J.M. Swales, compilers, 1999–2000.

Finally, thank you to my husband, Amir, and my children, Rosteen and Leyla, for your love, support, and patience.

Contents

Unit 3   Understanding Lecture Organizational Elements and Other Features of Lectures   73

Additional Practice Section   123

Appendixes   141

Table of Strategies

Chart of Video and Audio Clips

Chart of Video and Audio Clips, Unit 1

Clip #	Description	Purpose	Tasks	Duration	Due date
1	Rosenthal: An Overview of the American Healthcare System	diagnostic	Unit 1, Tasks 1, 2 Unit 2, Task 11	11:39	
2	Student: Kong	lecture culture differences	Unit 1, Task 11	3:40	
3 audio only	MICASE: BIO 152	an interactive lecture	Unit 1, Tasks 12,13 Unit 2, Task 10	7:02	
4	Swales: Written and Spoken Grammar	a closed style	Unit 1, Task 14	3:46	
5	Swales: Written and Spoken Grammar	an open style	Unit 1, Task 14	4:30	
6	Student: Nam	office hours strategy	Unit 1, Tasks 17, 18	2:00	

Chart of Video and Audio Clips, Unit 2

Clip #	Description	Purpose	Tasks	Duration	Due date
7 audio only	MICASE Advising Session	messiness of spoken language	Unit 2, Tasks 4, 9	1:31	
8	Rosenthal: Short Excerpt	stress placement	Unit 2, Tasks 7, 8, 9	1:09	
9	Student: Xiaoyu	preparation strategy	Unit 2, Task 12	2:07	
10	Swales: History of English, Part 1	headings	Unit 2, Task 13	5:25	
11	Swales: History of English, Part 2	headings	Unit 2, Task 14	7:17	
12	Carvajal: Intro to Agroecology	background, predicting, visuals, topic change	Unit 2, Tasks 15, 16, 17 Unit 3, Tasks 23, 26, 27	34:21	
13 audio only	MICASE Addictive Drugs Intro.	introduction	Unit 2, Tasks 18, 19, 20 21, 22	2:14	
14	Pollack: Global AIDS	introduction, humor	Unit 2, Task 23 Unit 3, Tasks 31, 33	5:39	
15	Mathews: Campus Safety	Unit 2 review	Unit 2, Task 29	6:53	

Chart of Video and Audio Clips, Unit 3

Clip #	Description	Purpose	Tasks	Duration	Due date
16	Winful: What's a Laser? Part 1	micro element	Unit 3, Tasks 4, 5, 6, 7, 12	23:13	
17	Winful: What's a Laser? Part 2	extra practice topic change	Unit 3, Tasks 8, 9, 25	26:30	
18	Alpine: Introduction to Prosthodontics	definitions, process description, visuals	Unit 3, Tasks 13, 14, 15, 24	14:49	
19 audio only	MICASE: Radiological Health Engineering	digression	Unit 3, Tasks 34, 35, 36	6:23	

Chart of Video and Audio Clips, Additional Practice Section

Clip #	Description	Purpose	Tasks	Duration	Due date
20	Rosenthal: Part 2	extra practice	Practice Unit, Task 2	7:30	
21	Rosenthal: Part 3	extra practice	Practice Unit, Task 3	13:12	
22	Rosenthal: Part 4	extra practice summary hedging	Unit 2, Task 27 Unit 3, Tasks 17, 18 Practice Unit, Tasks 4, 5	7:39	
23	Deardorff: International Trade and Less-Developed Countries	extra practice	Practice Unit, Task 6	50:22	

Introduction for the Student

Some Things to Think about Before You Use This Text

Given the importance of lectures as a means of instruction in your academic coursework, it is critical for you, the student, to be aware of *what* is being conveyed, *how* it is conveyed, and *what* you can do to improve your comprehension. Yet understanding lectures is indeed very difficult, and your understanding probably varies depending on the context and the speaker. Why is this so true? What characteristics of lectures and speakers influence your comprehension? And what can you do to improve your lecture comprehension?

This textbook is designed to help make the comprehension process more manageable. As you work through this text and the video material, you will begin to see features of lectures that can aid your understanding. In addition, you will become familiar with a variety of comprehension strategies and be given opportunities to practice strategies for:

- preparing for lectures
- listening better during lectures
- recognizing what information you have missed
- compensating for information you missed with methods other than reading and rereading the assigned texts

You begin by taking an inventory of the strategies you have used to understand lectures in your previous educational experiences to take advantage of what you already do well. You will then be introduced to a wider variety of strategies so that you can practice using those that are most effective for you. You will also begin to better understand how lecture culture can vary and will examine the expectations you have about lectures based on your previous educational experiences.

In Unit 2, you will be introduced to some key features of spoken English. Understanding these features will help you to unscramble the stream of language that you hear. You will practice some helpful strategies such as listening to key words and using lecture introductions to predict lecture content.

In Unit 3 you will have a detailed look at common patterns in lectures, and you will practice some strategies to help when you encounter definitions, opinions, and jokes. In the Additional Practice Section, you will have an opportunity to apply what you have learned to other lecture material.

The exercises in this text, together with the lectures and short talks on the DVDs and your classroom instruction, will provide you with many lecture-listening opportunities to practice effective listening strategies. The video component includes four entire lectures, as well as several lecture segments and shorter informal talks. Also included are short audio selections of academic speech from the Michigan Corpus of Academic Spoken English (MICASE). For additional information see *www.lsa.umich.edu/eli/micase/index.htm*). These selections demonstrate actual and authentic academic speech in university lectures.

By becoming aware of the characteristics of academic lectures featured in this text and by practicing new strategies while listening to the many audio and video segments provided on the DVDs, you will be able to improve your comprehension of academic lectures.

Introduction for the Teacher

These materials have been designed for intermediate and advanced English language students who are currently or will soon be enrolled in English-medium college or university coursework but need additional listening comprehension practice as well as more effective strategies for understanding lectures. This text is accompanied by audio/visual material in DVD format (for classroom or individual use).

In the past ten years, a number of researchers have identified specific lecture characteristics that students should be aware of, and researchers have indicated the skills that students need to have to understand lectures better.[1] This textbook reflects much of the current research on academic listening, including:

- attention to both top-down and bottom-up processing strategies
- variety of video examples of naturally occurring speech from lecture situations
- a few audio examples from the Michigan Corpus of Academic Spoken English (MICASE)
- four full-length, authentic lectures for practice understanding whole lectures
- attention to patterns in lectures
- attention to speaker purpose and the structure of utterances
- attention to important aspects of academic culture that may differ from students' previous educational experiences, for example, the interactive nature of many lectures
- strategies in note taking, such as abbreviating, organizing, and compensating for what was missed
- an emphasis on awareness of one's strategies and their effectiveness
- offering students access to video materials (as a companion to the textbook)

Unit 1 begins with a description of the complexity of lecture comprehension and a diagnostic exercise to help you and the students identify areas of lecture comprehension that may be most difficult for them. Students then assess which strategies they are cur-

---

[1]Flowerdew, *Academic Listening: Research Perspectives.*

rently using and which ones might be useful to try. Unit 1 draws attention to cultural aspects of lectures—such as the interactive nature of many lectures and typical student and professor behavior during lectures—and it reinforces the idea that using office hours to compensate for what is missed in a lecture can be helpful.

Unit 2 opens with a discussion of the idea that written English and spoken English are very different and then focuses on the bottom-up features (or sound and word-level patterns) present in everyday spoken English. Unit 2 addresses aspects of fast speech such as linking, reduction, and blending as they occur in spoken English. Students are taught to listen for stressed elements, to listen to whole phrases, and to focus on redundancy in naturally occurring speech to help them understand spoken English better. Unit 2 then addresses top-down processing strategies for listening to lectures, such as getting background information, processing structural cues, and focusing on introductions and summaries to understand the main ideas.

Unit 3 focuses on patterns that can be found in lectures and includes an emphasis on both top-down and bottom-up processing. First, students will look at some macro patterns commonly used to organize whole lectures. Then students will look at several common micro elements, including definitions and process descriptions. Strategies for dealing with the simultaneous presentation of spoken text with visual material are addressed as well as how a speaker's level of formality or informality may affect listeners. Other aspects of lectures that students typically have difficulties with are also addressed, including the use of humor in lectures.

The Additional Practice Unit is designed to provide students who want extra practice with more opportunities to listen to lectures and more opportunities to practice new strategies. You may assign these exercises to a subgroup of the class or you may decide to assign these as extra homework for all students. I assign the Rosenthal segments in the Additional Practice Unit to all students in the first three weeks of class because it is important to have listened to the entire lecture at the point when summary statements are discussed at the end of Unit 2. I have found that the Deardorff segment is most useful, however, as a final assignment at the end of the term.

In my classroom, I assign most of the video clips as homework (except for the diagnostic, which I do in class), to be done either on a PC/Mac at home or in a computer lab equipped with headphones. This allows more class time for pair work and whole-class discussion, and it allows time for attention to individual needs. I do show shorter clips from the DVDs in class, to reinforce the main purpose of the assignments. Be sure to watch the clips yourself before you plan to use them in class so you know exactly what is on them and so that you can better anticipate student responses. You will also want to add your own ideas to those offered in the Answer Key (available online). I also try to augment these video lectures with a couple of live lectures, especially toward the latter half of the course, to provide students with opportunities to interact with the lecturer and to provide a richer lecture context.

Students are directed to keep a listening journal (p. 10) to help them reflect more deeply on the effectiveness of the strategies they are using and to reinforce awareness of the learning process. Student journals can provide you with important insight into student progress. They can be collected periodically, and you can give guidance directly in the journal, in class, or during office hours.

Instructions for Using the DVDs

One of the main goals of these materials is to provide students with their own access to the listening materials. Students often ask for more listening practice; they often want to listen to a single segment multiple times, and these materials are designed to allow for this kind of individual use. DVDs allow for repeated use without wear, as well as the ability to locate a specific segment quickly, which makes them superior to VHS. Students then use DVD materials for homework assignments either in a language or computer lab or at their own personal computers. We recommend that a language department purchase a class set of DVDs for students to use at home or in a language or computer lab, but students may want to purchase their own copies.

My experience playing the DVDs in class has shown me that TV/DVD players and remote controllers operate slightly differently from each other. As a result, I strongly recommend that instructors become familiar with the *exact machines* that they will be using in class. Advance planning strategies—such as practicing playing the appropriate clip before class and locating the position of the *Pause* and *Rewind* buttons on the remote control that you will use—will make playing the clips in class much easier. One important feature you will need to operate is the *Counter.* DVD remotes allow you to put a counter on the screen so that you can start and stop very precisely. You will need to know how to operate this feature before using the equipment in class. Times indicated are total running time from the beginning of each DVD. The text includes segments for those exercises requiring precision timing so that if you don't have a counter available, you can still do the exercises easily. Also, if you are timing from the beginning of the clip, text is provided to assist you in locating the particular point of interest. Note also that the textual material that appears on the DVD during lectures represents material originally written on the board or OHP.

Instructions for Computer Users

For Users with a PC:

1. Open your DVD software application.

2. Insert the DVD.

3. Use the mouse to select "play."

4. To return to the DVD menu, select the DVD button with the mouse and select "DVD menu."

5. Double-click on the title of the lecture you want to play.

6. Two numbers appear at the bottom of the screen. The first number is the counter that shows where you are on that DVD; the second number is the total playing time of that DVD.

For Users with a Mac:

1. When you insert your DVD, your DVD application should automatically open.

2. Use the mouse to select "play."

3. To return to the DVD menu, select the DVD button with the mouse and select "DVD menu."

4. Double-click on the title of the lecture you want to play.

5. Two numbers appear at the bottom of the screen. The first number is the counter that shows where you are on that DVD, the second number is the total playing time of that DVD.

Some Comments about the Video and Audio Material

Every effort has been made in the creation of these materials to include a variety of authentic academic speech events and speakers. Included are formal lectures, interactive lecture segments, informal "talks," an academic advising session, and brief interview segments. Though the majority of professors are from North America, two British English speakers are featured, as well as one professor and three students for whom English is a second language.

Four audio-only MICASE segments are also included because it has always been my goal to prepare students to deal with the real-world demands of lecture comprehension through exposure to lecture situations that come as close as possible to real-world events. As is typical for instructors of lecture comprehension courses, I have in the past typically invited live lecturers to visit my classes, I have taken classes on excursions to listen to lectures, and have used a variety of videotaped material. I was, in fact, strongly prejudiced against material that was audio-only, maintaining that academic listening commonly involves a visual of some kind. I did not use audio-only material in my earlier teaching because I thought it was less representative of the real situations students face.

However, when the MICASE project began down the hall from my office in 1998, I began to read lecture transcripts from the corpus and discovered that the lectures I had been using in class had some striking differences from the ones recorded on audio from actual class situations found in the MICASE corpus. I realized that the speakers who came to lecture for my classes showed a degree of sensitivity to their audience that I did not find common in MICASE; they often slowed their speech, used clear examples, and often refrained from using a lot of idiomatic expressions or jokes. They couldn't refer to other texts beyond the assigned reading for that lecture since students did not have any other texts in common. The MICASE corpus data, on the other hand, revealed more complex and difficult lecture listening scenarios—such as more rapid delivery of information, more references to historical events that were not within the students' knowledge base, and more frequent use of idioms. I realized that my videos and lectures had brought a *simplified* real-world to my classroom. And while some simplification can be helpful initially, exposing students only to simplified lecture texts certainly does students a disservice. Exposing students to a fuller range of complex discourse that they will most likely encounter in their academic careers is, in my opinion, of great value. Clearly, preparing students for the challenges they will face with the Next Generation TOEFL® or iBT® lecture comprehension section will require instructors to be aware of the complexity in academic lectures, and students will need to practice with texts of equal complexity.

I still consider the visual component to be a vital part of academic lecture listening instruction, as is demonstrated in the inclusion of 19 video segments. However, I have come to see great value also in the audio-only material available in the MICASE corpus. The four audio segments and their transcripts included in this text demonstrate some very rich and complex authentic uses of academic English. For example, the academic advising session, Clip 7, is valuable as an eye-opener and helps students begin to see why they have such trouble understanding some of the casual speech spoken around them. The richness of the text, the false starts, the incomplete utterances, the slang and blending of sounds speak volumes—even without a dynamic visual component. It is my view now that the authentic and rich nature of the interactions more than compensate for the lack of a video component.

Note also that in authentic lectures, material is sometimes included, such as a joke, that could only be understood by the original audience. Therefore, some very minor editing of three or four clips became necessary. In Clips 10 and 11, for example, you may notice a few edits. We believe these edits do not interfere with the overall usefulness of the material.

UNIT 1

Lecture Culture and Your Listening Strategies

In this unit you will:

- think about the complexity of lecture comprehension
- assess your strengths and weaknesses
- inventory strategies you have used in the past
- practice using new strategies, such as listening to headings (speaker announcements of purpose and topics)
- look at some important aspects of lecture culture
- learn the importance of listening broadly
- increase your awareness of accuracy, organization and abbreviations in your notes
- understand your role in continuing to develop strategies for listening

Another intended outcome:

- you will gain confidence that good listening skills are achievable

1

You have probably recognized that lecture comprehension is a very complex process. In fact, it is one of the most linguistically demanding challenges you will face. To help you understand just how complex it is, a list of many of the challenges a student faces while listening to a lecture follows.

Some Unique Challenges of Lecture Listening

- Multiple sources of input—audio and visual—must be simultaneously attended to, filtered, and written down in real time.
- The spoken text disappears after you hear it, unlike a written text.
- Great variety exists across disciplines, courses, lecturers, and even subject matter.
- Opportunities to get more explanation or react may need to be delayed.
- References to cultural elements outside the non-native English speaker's background are plentiful.
- Lecturers invite input from students who may be harder to understand.
- Lecturer opinions may not be stated in an obvious manner.
- Listeners need to guess a speaker's purpose and intentions when they are not directly stated.
- Lecturers may change topics without clear signaling.
- A whole set of new abbreviations for note taking may need to be developed for each course.
- Lecturers may speak with an accent with which you are unfamiliar.
- Terms will be introduced that you don't know how to spell.

You will certainly encounter some of these difficulties whenever you listen to spoken English. The challenge with lectures is that you have to master your course content in spite of these challenges, and you usually need to take notes to help you remember the content.

To help you determine what you already do well and what areas you still need to work on, we will begin with a diagnostic exercise where you will listen to the first part of a lecture, take notes, and answer some questions. You will be listening to a ten-minute excerpt of a lecture. Professor Rosenthal is speaking on the topic of the U.S. health-care system and giving some cultural background to international students. This lecture was recorded in 1998. Though some comments are dated, the issues she discusses are very current.

TASK 1

STEP 1

Before listening to any lecture, it is important to consider what you may already know about the subject. Spending some time thinking about what you know and predicting what you will hear is a vital before-lecture strategy because it helps to prepare you for what you will hear. The more prepared you are, the more you will be able to understand.

1. Professor Rosenthal is a medical sociologist—a scholar who studies the interaction of society and different parts of our healthcare system, such as hospitals, doctors, other medical personnel, insurance companies, and so forth. Based on this information, what expectations do you have in regard to the content of this lecture? How might she approach the topic as a sociologist? Would you expect a broad coverage of the topic, or would you expect her to cover a narrow topic, in an "overview"?

_____

_____

_____

_____

2. What are some of the most important healthcare issues in the United States that you have heard or read about? For example, you might have heard something about the high costs of medical care in the United States or the high number of uninsured Americans.

_____

_____

_____

_____

STEP 2

Listen to Part 1 of the lecture one time (DVD 1, Clip 1, Professor Rosenthal), taking notes from the very beginning of the lecture as if you were in the class. Before Professor Rosenthal begins to speak, you will see some information on a screen and will need to decide if you should copy it into your notes. This is the information Professor Rosenthal wrote on the board. Be sure to write any notes on a full sheet of paper. You will use your notes to answer comprehension questions, and the answers and your notes will help you discover what elements in a lecture you might need to pay more attention to.

STEP 3

After you have listened to Part 1 one time, answer these questions. Use your notes to help you.

Listening Diagnostic— Rosenthal Lecture, Part I

Preparation/Orientation

1. What is the title of the lecture? (1 pt)

Introductory Remarks

2. What three characteristics are reflected in all major institutions? (3 pts)

   • _____

   • _____

   • _____

Detail

3. What is an example of an institution mentioned other than healthcare? (1 pt)

Definition

4. What does *heterogeneous* mean? (1 pt)

Main Idea/Organization

5. What are three important features/characteristics of American healthcare? (3 pts)

   - _____

   - _____

   - _____

Organization

6. What is one element of "individualism" that is mentioned? (1 pt)

Completeness/Detail

7. What do Americans think about "choice"? (1 pt)

Detail

8. Why aren't there many for-profit hospitals in Michigan? (1 pt)

Detail

9. What is one example of a for-profit enterprise in the private sector? (1 pt)

Detail

10. What is one responsibility/goal of for-profit hospitals? (1pt)

Main Idea

11. What are the biggest sources of money for medical research? (2 pts)

   - _____

   - _____

Opinion

12. Which aspect of the American healthcare system does Professor Rosenthal think is the most important? (2 pts)

Total Points: _____

Using the Diagnostic

In this diagnostic exercise, the questions are focused on the main idea, details and opinions to help you get an idea of what you might need to work on. Sometimes getting the details can be easier than understanding the main idea because details are smaller units of information. You might understand them but have trouble understanding *how* the details provide support to a larger idea. If this is the case for you, you may be focusing too narrowly on what you hear. Additionally, noting the instructor's emphasis on a particular point or understanding his or her opinion can be difficult. Maybe you noticed the emphasis or opinion but failed to record it in your notes. Since lecturers convey emphasis and opinions as well as factual information, noticing and recording these elements is also very important.

TASK 2

STEP 1

Look at the sample notes for this lecture introduction (Appendix C, pp. 145–46). Compare them to yours in terms of:

- completeness
- accuracy
- use of abbreviations
- noting emphasis and opinions
- overall organization
- use of space (white space, arrows, boxes)

1. What are some differences between your notes and the sample notes? Compare your notes to a partner's notes. Discuss the differences.

_____

_____

_____

2. Based on this information, write in the space what you personally should focus on improving with regard to taking notes. For example, should you try to use more abbreviations? (For some ideas on abbreviating common terms, see Appendix A, p. 142.)

_____

_____

_____

STEP 2

Let's return to the beginning of the diagnostic video (Clip 1, Professor Rosenthal, Part 1). Listen as many times as you need in order to understand what you may have missed. Analyze any incorrect or incomplete answers from the diagnostic. Make a list describing reasons for each incorrect answer. For example,

1. I missed the first question because I wasn't thinking this information could be important.

2. I missed question 9 because I was stuck on the word _pharmaceutical_ and missed the details that followed.

Note: The practice unit beginning on page 123 included exercises for the rest of Professor Rosenthal's lecture. This lecture has been divided into three more short parts that can be found on DVD 3, Practice Unit, Clips 20, 21, and 22. The exercises and the video clips provide additional practice for you to listen for the main ideas, details, emphasis, and opinions. If you struggled with understanding this first portion of the lecture—if you got fewer than 14 points on the diagnostic—you should listen to all three of these sections and do the extra practice exercises in the first two weeks of your class. If you got 14 points or more on the diagnostic, you may choose to do these exercises if you want more practice.

To help you further analyze your strengths and weaknesses in relation to lecture comprehension, discuss the form in Appendix B, pages 143–44.

Personal Strategy Inventory

TASK 3

Look at the following list of strategies. Identify the strategies _you typically use_ when listening to a lecture or informal talk _in your first language_ (or the language you have used most commonly in academic situations). Place an F for _first academic language_ in front of each item on the list. Then identify with an E the strategies _you typically use_ when listening to a lecture or informal talk _in English_.

Before Class

_____ Read the assigned material before class.

_____ Review what you already know about the lecture topic.

_____ Make informed guesses about the content/approach of the lecture.

_____ Discuss the topic with classmates.

_____ Create a list of questions about the topic.

_____ Create a list of new terms from the reading material.

_____ Reflect on previous lectures in this class.

_____ Get to class early and begin to predict what the lecture will be about.

_____ Other: _____.

In Class

_____ Take notes.

_____ Use the speaker's introduction to make predictions/develop a framework.

_____ Listen without taking notes.

_____ Recognize the speaker's organizational patterns.

_____ Use visual cues (hand gestures, facial expressions) to aid comprehension.

_____ Tape-record lecture for later listening (obtain permission first).

_____ Write notes on the handouts.

_____ Use language cues (e.g., *now we will move on to the next topic*).

_____ Notice and record instructor emphasis/opinions in your notes.

_____ Other: _____.

After Class

_____ Ask questions after the lecture.

_____ Remain in your seat and write more while the information is fresh.

_____ Use office hours to discuss any problems you had.

_____ Read or reread the assigned material.

_____ Highlight the main ideas in your notes.

_____ Summarize the main ideas from the lecture.

_____ Copy another student's notes.

_____ Discuss the lecture with others.

_____ Other: _____.

Evaluating Your Progress

_____ Indicate in the notes where you missed information.

_____ Notice areas for improvement.

_____ Keep a journal of your progress (see p. 10).

_____ Other: _____.

Are there any strategies that you used in your past academic experience that you are not using now? Can you explain to a partner why not?

_____

_____

_____

_____

_____

TASK 4

What strategies do you think are most important? Indicate those with an I. Which ones are most difficult for you? Indicate those with a D. Are there any that might <u>not</u> be good to use in certain instances or at all? Discuss your lists with a partner.

_____

_____

_____

TASK 5

In a group, make a list of four or five strategies that should be used for every lecture. Have one member present this list to the class. Are there some strategies that your group listed that might be ideal to use but that few in the group actually use?

_____

_____

_____

_____

Evaluating Your Progress

Evaluating your progress is a helpful method for improving your lecture comprehension. Keeping a listening journal is one good way to evaluate the effectiveness of the strategies you are using and whether they help you. For this you will need to have a notebook in which you will write your reactions to the listening activities you do in the class and to the listening activities you do outside of class. You will write about how you are applying new strategies and to what extent they are working. The purpose of this journal is to demonstrate to you how much English you are or are not listening to, to aid you in discovering your strengths and weaknesses, and to help you see your progress.

In your journal you should comment on:

- the strategies you use for lectures and how they affect your comprehension
- your reactions to the listening activities you do in the class
- the strategies you use for the listening you do on your own outside of class

You should make entries several times each week, that could look like this:

July 1

I think I can understand about 60% of what my instructors say in class, but I am not sure how to compensate for what I miss. I can only understand about 20% of a TV program. Our instructor gave us some strategies for compensating today. I made a mark in my notes where I lost the speaker and missed information. Then I asked another student after class about what I missed. This method for compensating is useful for me, but sometimes I am not aware of what I miss. I need to find an additional compensating strategy.

July 3

Today we discussed the need for being prepared for our lectures. If we read ahead in the text and have adequate background on the material, this helps us with understanding the lecture information. I must prepare more before the lectures by previewing the material and developing expectations for the lecture. I have been reading the material after lecture. I will try this for the next lecture and report on the impact on my listening comprehension.

Be sure to be as specific as possible in your entries. Try to incorporate what is discussed in class. You do not need lengthy entries, but frequent ones are helpful.

TASK 6

Buy or create a notebook, and write your first entry describing what strategies you think you need to work on and why.

TASK 7

Select two strategies that you are going to work on in the next lecture. After you use the strategies, write a paragraph in your listening journal describing the ones you used and to what extent they influenced your lecture comprehension. For example, if you spent extra time reading the material before a lecture, report on how reading that material affected your comprehension of that lecture. Compare your notes for that lecture to notes you took when you did not read the material before the lecture. What do you notice? Do you notice that you are able to understand the main ideas better or to record more details? Are you more able to understand how the lecture is organized?

TASK 8

Report to your partner which strategies you used and how they affected your comprehension.

Your View of Lecture Listening

Now that you have begun to think about the strategies you use and to try out some new strategies, it's time to think more broadly about lecture listening and how you listen. Often students listen for small pieces of information, which is a good strategy because you need to understand small pieces of information. But if you listen too narrowly, only to these pieces, you may miss the main points that you need in order to make sense of the whole lecture. Listening too narrowly is like looking at the lecture with a microscope instead of with satellite photography. A microscope allows you to view something very, very closely; satellite photography allows you to view a very large region. When listening to a lecture, you need to get the details, <u>and</u> you need to get the big picture so that you can understand what the details mean. Therefore, you have to use strategies that help you with both broad and narrow listening.

Some students process the spoken texts of lectures using a local, word-by-word strategy—that is, they translate in their heads into their native language as they listen in English. This is a narrow focus that will hinder the understanding of the larger picture. First of all, translating slows you down so you will miss information as you translate and as the speaker keeps talking. Second, as shown in Unit 2, there are many features of spoken English that create significant difficulties for someone who is trying to translate (see pp. 34–41).

To summarize:

Broad Listening	Narrow Listening
think about topic first	translate word-by-word
listen for main idea	have to know every particle
do not listen to every word	miss larger picture
"satellite-view listening"	"microscope listening"

Do you have a broad focus or a narrow focus when listening in English? If you are translating into your native language when you listen in English, here are some ideas to help you listen more broadly:

1. Do as many of the before-lecture strategies (p. 8) as you can before the lecture.

2. Listen to English as often as you can.

   • Listen to the video clips for the exercises in this text several times.

   • Record a few lectures yourself (with the permission of the lecturer), and listen to them several times.

   • Listen to the radio daily, and discuss what you hear with a classmate.

Listen to English day and night, so that your ear and your brain become used to listening and thinking in English. Can you think of some other strategies that might help you to listen more broadly?

Assumptions You Might Have about Lecture Culture

You have already been studying for many years and as a result of your previous educational experiences, you have assumptions about what lecturers do and what lectures are like. However, assumptions about lecture culture may differ significantly. Since the assumptions you have will influence how you listen and which strategies you will use, it is a good idea to become familiar with the lecture culture you will be a part of so you can begin to adopt new strategies, if necessary, for the lectures you will encounter.

TASK 9

Two sets of assumptions about lecture culture follow. Discuss the assumptions in Boxes A and B with a partner. Which set of assumptions is more closely related to the academic culture you have experienced in the past? Which do you think are the assumptions in the country where you are currently studying?

_____

_____

_____

A	B
1. Lecturers do all the talking; students respectfully and silently receive the teacher's knowledge.	1. Lecturers evaluate ideas and expect students to react, analyze, and question in class.
2. Lecturers generally assume a central role with great authority.	2. Lecturers and students have ideas to share with each other.
3. When taking notes, students should write down as much as they can as fast as they can— understanding can come later.	3. The instructor may assume the role of facilitator, mentor, or participant.
4. If something was not clear in the lecture, it is most often due to the student's inability to understand the lecture material.	4. When taking notes, a student is expected to evaluate the material, show relationships between ideas, and indicate missing information.
5. The lecturer may give an opinion; the student is not free to challenge it.	5. If something was not clear, it may be due to the speaker or the listener.
6. The lecturer may read the lecture.	6. The listener may be invited to interrupt the lecture for clarification or to ask a question.
7. The student-teacher relationship is typically characterized by formality and a degree of distance.	7. Listening to a lecturer is somewhat like listening to a person talk casually, but with important subject matter.
	8. Graduate students may address the lecturer by his or her first name.

The assumptions in Box B reflect some of the ideas about lectures and lecturers that are common in the United States and Canada, as well as some other countries. As you progress through this book, you will become more familiar with aspects of this lecture culture. For example, in Task 12 you will listen to an audio clip of an interactive class where the instructor expects students to help construct a definition. This is an example of the kind of interactivity that is becoming increasingly common in many classrooms, especially in the United States, but also elsewhere. In Unit 2, you will have a look at some of the informal features of spoken English that are present in lectures.

It's important to recognize that you will probably need to consider adapting the lecture comprehension strategies that you have used in the past in order to adjust to your new lecture culture. If you are used to hearing only the professor talk in a lecture class, for example, you may need to be ready with new strategies for listening to other students. Increasingly, especially in smaller classes, lecturers may move from the expected format of "professor talks and student listens" and incorporate student input into the lecture or sometimes break the class into small groups for discussion, after which some students may report to the class. (These types of lectures are featured on the Next Generation TOEFL® Test.) These alternative class structures reflect an educational philosophy that encourages students to be full participants, to be inquiring, and to be constantly interacting with the material, not just absorbing information. However, these alternative class formats place an additional listening burden on international students. It's often harder to understand classmates than the professor!

One strategy to deal with the group-work class format is to let a classmate in your group know that you have some trouble understanding the group discussion. Ask that classmate if he or she could summarize the main points of the discussion for the group or for you privately. Or, if they take notes in discussion, ask if you could borrow or make a copy of the notes.

TASK 10

Evaluate the B list on page 14 with regard to the strategies you would need to be able to take a more active role in your classes. Review the strategy list on pages 8–9, and write in the margin of the page the strategies that would be helpful for each point on the lists. For example, if instructors expect students to react in class, then extra preparation before class is necessary. You would write *prepare before class* next to Point 1 in Box B.

In the next task you will hear about one student's personal experience with differences between his home lecture culture and the one he encountered in the United States and his reflections about these differences.

TASK 11

Watch DVD 1, Clip 2. Kong, a graduate student in epidemiology, will talk about some differences in lecture culture between China and the United States. What are the two differences he mentions? Have you had similar experiences? What other differences in lecture culture have you noticed between your present host culture and your previous experience in other academic cultures? Discuss your answers with a classmate.

_____

_____

_____

_____

_____

_____

Next you will hear a small portion of a lecture given to a group of undergraduates on the first day of a biology course, and you will have an opportunity to hear a sample of how informal and interactive American lecture culture can be. This lecture material was taken from the MICASE corpus, which is a collection of authentic academic speech samples recorded for research purposes to help us understand academic speech better. This lecture segment (Clip 3) is available on audio only.

In this portion of the biology lecture the professor is creating a definition of what it means to be "alive." He elicits various characteristics of living organisms from the students and discusses *metabolism,* which has to do with the process of converting food into energy. (As a cultural note, he attempts to use humor to illustrate his point. Some may not think his use of humor in this instance is appropriate.) He spends a long time developing the definition while inviting student help. The pace is rather slow at times because the professor writes on an overhead as he talks.

TASK 12

STEP 1

Listen to DVD 1, Clip 3, at least twice.

The second time you listen, take notes as if you were in the class. Share your notes with a classmate. What was the most important information? What did you not need to record in your notes?

STEP 2

Compare your notes with the sample notes (in Appendix C, pp. 146–47). Be sure to look at:

- accuracy
- completeness
- organization
- use of abbreviations

STEP 3

Why do you think the professor didn't simply give a straightforward definition of how biologists define "being alive"? What do you think his purpose is in this portion of the lecture?

_____

_____

_____

STEP 4

After you have listened to the segment at least two times, listen while reading the following transcript. For now, ignore the fact that some words appear in boldfaced type. You will come back to those in Unit 2.

MICASE BIO 152 First Day of Class

1 Professor: **Biology**, simple **definition here**, is just

2 the **study** of **life**. So, that, **begs** the **question**... what is **alive**?... okay who's **gonna give**

3 **me** a **definition** of **what's alive**?

4 Student 1: **things** that, **react** and **reproduce**

5 Professor: **react**, and **reproduce**. Do you have a **grandmother**?

6 Student 1: Yeah

7 Professor: Is she **reproducing**?

8 Student 1: **Not lately**.

9 Professor: Is **she alive**?

10 Student 1: Yeah

11 Professor: So **your definition doesn't work**. So **she's dead** she's you you're

12 **happy** to **redefine** her as **dead**?

13 Student 1: uh... maybe I **should've said** the **possibility** of **reproducing**

14 Professor: **Capable** of **reproducing**? At **some point** in her **life cycle**?

15 Student 1: Right

16 Professor: I **mean** the **same goes true** for **priests** and **nuns** and, and **capable** of

17 **reproducing**... at **some point. What** do you **mean by react**, or **somebody else** what

18 does he **mean** by **react**? **Poke** her with a **stick** and she **yells** at you?... **has** to be **able**

19 to **respond**, to, **environment**. Okay. **What** are **other properties** I **mean** what it's

20 **coming down** to is we're gonna, **not really have one easy definition** of **alive** and **not**

21 **alive**. What we're gonna **end up doing** is just, **coming up** with a **bunch** of **properties**

22 of **living organisms**.

23 So **what** are **other properties** of **living organisms**? I know you were **all made** to

24 **memorize this** in **seventh grade**.

25 Student 2: **consume energy**

26 Professor: **consume energy**. Okay... **who else**?

27 Student 3: **made** of **cells**.

28 Professor: **Made** of **cells**, okay... **that's** at **least true**, for **everything**

29 **we know** on **this planet**, that there **living creatures** are uh, **made** of **cells**... alright.

30 **See** what **I've got** on **my list**... **I've got**... well I I'll just **give you my list** and and

31 we'll **see, how much** that **overlaps metabolism**... **I've got growth** and

32 **reproduction**... so, **growth** in **size and growth** in **number**... and **then I've got**

33 **evolution**... and, **adaptation**. Okay? So, **adaptation** is **basically, responding** to your

34 **environment. Metabolism** is, **all** the **reactions** that **you do** to, **gather energy** from

35 the **environment** and **convert** it, **into,** uh, **useful, compounds**. um... **Made** of **cells**

36 **like I said** is **how life is** on **this, planet** it's sort of a **consequence** of what's **happened**

37 in **evolution,** here. and **reproduction** we've also **got covered**. Okay?

38 **My** sort of**, semi-solid definition of life, would be**... **anything, that can convert,**

39 **materials from its environment into, more copies of itself**.... okay? So **you have**

40 to be **able** to **take those things, those sugars those chemicals those, buildi-** those

41 **ions those building blocks** that are **out there,** and **convert them** that's the

42 **metabolism part,** into **more copies** of **itself**. So, it it **makes more** of **itself** and

43 **increases** in **number,** um, the **fact,** well, I- **living organisms have to be** able to

44 **respond** to their **environment** to **either move away** from **bad things** or **move**

45 **towards,** uh, t- t- to **be able** to **find more** and **collect more materials from** its

46 **environment**. And it's **also** an **inevitable consequence** that in **making copies** of

47 **themselves,** they **don't make perfect copies, therefore** the **subsequent generations**

48 **change** and there's **evolution**.

49 Student 4: Would you say that **has** to **be,** a **natural, occurrence**? I **mean** wh- **when**

50 **you say convert** it **makes me think** of **cloning. We've,** you know, **we've talked**

51 **about science** as um **taking materials** and **making copies** of its um **ourselves**.

52 Professor: Okay, or **cloning would be reproducing,** I- in a **sense** it's **asexual**

53 **reproduction,** but, **even cloning would not work** if the **cell could not carry out**

54 **metabolism,** to **make** the **proteins** that that **second cell** or that **second organism**

55 **needs,** the the **membranes** the **ribosomes** the **D-N-A** the **R-N-A**. So, **cloning does**

56 **require,** um **metabolism** and **growth** in **size before** you can **split** into **two cells** or

57 **two organisms,** which would be then **asexual reproduction**. So, **cloning does fit**

58 **under** sort of, **creation** of **new life**.

59 Y- **you** can **think** of **lots** of **things** like the **classic example is: Is a virus alive**? And

60 **my opinion** is **no** it's **not, because** it **cannot metabolize unless it infects** a **cell** and

61 **convinces** the **cell** to do the **metabolizing for it**. But **things like apple seeds** which,

62 **remain dormant** and **essentially**, are **doing very little** if **any metabolism**. **Are they**

63 **alive**? *Well, I guess we would say yes* because they're **capable** of **metabolism** and

64 **capable** of **growth** and **reproduction under** the **right conditions**.

65 Student 5: **What about** like a **person** in a **coma**?

66 **person** in a **coma** is, **still metabolizing**, and, um

67 Student 5: **They can't do anything** with the **environment** um,

68 Professor: **That's, correct** and **now we're getting into** sort of **sticky philosophical**

69 and **legal definitions**….

Source: Used with permission from R. C. Simpson, S. L. Briggs, J. Ovens, and J. M. Swales. *The Michigan Corpus of Academic Spoken English.* Ann Arbor: The Regents of the University of Michigan, 1999.

STEP 5

What cultural elements surprise you in this lecture? Discuss your answers with a partner.

- Do the professor's jokes about grandmothers reproducing or about poking a grandmother with a stick surprise you?

- Does the professor's directness (Line 11, "so your definition doesn't work") surprise you?

- In Lines 49 and 65, students interrupt and ask a question of the professor. Does this surprise you? Do they appear to be challenging the professor, or do you think they are simply showing their own interest in the development of the definition? What is his reaction to their questions?

TASK 13

Discuss these questions with a classmate.

1. This portion of the biology class is interactive. The professor is inviting student input. Do you think he is expecting the first student he calls on to give a complete "textbook" definition?

_____

_____

2. How could you characterize the student responses to his questions in terms of length?

3. Have you witnessed these kinds of opportunities for interaction in a lecture?

4. Do you volunteer answers when the professor asks questions? Why or why not?

Additional language issues with regard to this lecture will be discussed in Unit 2.

More about Lecture Culture

Open Lecture Style

Especially in the United States, but also elsewhere today, there is a tendency for lecturers to adopt what Swales[1] has referred to as an "open" lecture style. This means that lecturers generally do not read a lecture from a written text; instead they speak from notes or an outline. As a result, much of what they say is constructed on the spot, although the ideas themselves and the organization have been prepared ahead of time. This format has some advantages for the listeners. It allows the speaker and audience to have a more direct connection since the speaker is free to adapt the content depending on how it is received. For example, if students look confused, the speaker can give another example and check for understanding afterward or paraphrase what was said previously. Another advantage for listeners is that this more open style slows the flow of information, since the speaker has to think of how to shape his or her ideas, usually pausing often to think. Pauses slow the speed of information delivery, and this aids comprehension; listeners are given time to process what is being said during the pauses. Additionally, the open lecture style generally allows for a more interesting delivery because the speaker is aware of audience feedback and wants to create an atmosphere that compels the listeners to continue listening.

However, this open lecture style also presents some challenges for the listener: more ungrammatical phrases appear, more informal terms are used, and things are said that don't necessarily fit what we might have predicted. As was evident from the BIO 152 example, the interactive nature of a lecture can also be difficult for a listener to follow because you may not hear what other students say or you may not understand what they say. We will look more carefully at many of the language features that are present in this open style in Unit 2.

---

[1]Swales, *Research Genres: Explorations and Applications.*

Examine the first five minutes of a lecture presented in both a somewhat closed style (read from a text) and an open style (presented from an outline). Professor John Swales, Professor of Linguistics at the University of Michigan and noted expert on academic writing and academic speaking, will talk about some grammar differences between written and spoken English. The same information is conveyed in both examples.

TASK 14

Listen to DVD 1, Clip 4, and then to DVD 1, Clip 5. Compare these two presentations, and discuss the differences you noticed with a partner. In which presentation did Professor Swales appear to be more connected to the audience? In your opinion, which presentation was a more effective presentation of the material? Have you encountered either of these two styles of presenting in your previous educational experience?

_____

_____

_____

_____

Some strategies that may help when you encounter an open style lecture are the following:

- Read the background material before the lecture/interaction.
- Listen broadly, and try not to translate.
- Sit in the front of the class (if you sit near the speaker and he or she can hear a question or comment from another student, you are more likely to hear it as well).
- Compensate for what you miss by comparing your notes with a classmate after class.
- Involve yourself in informal interactions in English as much as possible to get practice.
- Stay focused so that longer pauses and extra examples are beneficial to you.

Professorial Behavior?

Another aspect of lecture culture you may encounter in some English-speaking countries includes what you might think of as *non-professorial behavior*. You might notice that some professors wear casual clothes; they may even wear jeans, tennis shoes, or sandals when they teach. You might notice professors drinking water, coffee, or soda while lecturing. They might even sit on top of a table or desk as they talk. These are behaviors that might surprise you, but they are considered quite normal, at least in North America. In Clip 5 you can see that Professor Swales has jeans on.

Many professors in the United States are likely to address their students by their first names, and professors of graduate students often encourage their students to address them by their first names. (A professor who wishes to be called by his or her first name will tell you directly. If you are not sure, do what other students do, or ask the professor.) The use of first names is an attempt to equalize the relationship and to reduce some of the stress that may be present in relationships where there is a difference in power. Of course, there is a difference in power between you and your professors, but the signals indicating this difference may be hard to notice with some professors.

Listener Behavior

Differences in audience behavior in academic cultures exist as well. You may already have noticed some differences if you have attended lectures with students from your host culture. Most lecturers in the United States will accept students eating and drinking as long as it is done quietly. It is understood that students might need to eat or drink something since most students have busy schedules. In Great Britain or Australia, it may be acceptable to drink something in a lecture, but it is not acceptable to eat. You will probably also notice some interesting postures among students in the U.S. university courses. Students might put their feet on the chair in front of them while they take notes. This would be unthinkable in many countries. While some people would consider this behavior to be too casual for a lecture situation, it would not generally be considered an insult to the speaker, at least in the United States.

However, one thing that is not acceptable in nearly all English-speaking countries is sleeping in class. In some cultures it may be fairly common to find a student sleeping through a lecture, but in North America, it is considered rude. Talking with your friends during a lecture is not acceptable in many countries either, unless you are talking about the content of the lecture and even that should be limited to brief comments.

TASK 15

Think about behavior that is considered acceptable and unacceptable for professors and for students to engage in during a lecture or class in your native country. Contrast that with what you have learned about the lecture culture behavior of your host culture. Make a list, and discuss it with some of your classmates.

TASK 16

If you are taking classes with students from your host culture, observe their behavior in class and note any differences from what you are accustomed to. Discuss your observations with a partner.

Office Hours

One more important aspect of lecture culture—that is often underutilized but available to you at North American, British, and Australian universities, as well as universities in other countries—is the opportunity to meet with your instructors during the time they have designated for individual student meetings. This time to meet with your instructors is called **office hours** and is the best time for you to ask questions about lecture material or anything related to class that you are having difficulty with and receive the instructor's private attention. If you try to ask the instructor immediately after class or in the hallway on the way to class, the instructor may not have time then to give you his or her complete attention. The privilege of using office hours is paid for/included in your tuition, and professors are expected to be available during the times they set as office hours. Office hours allow you to get valuable clarification of lecture material and also get to know your professors. Try to take advantage of this resource.

Often students whose native language is not English are concerned that their professor might not be able to understand them or that they might not be able to understand what the professor says, so they avoid making use of office hours. But, it's important to overcome these fears because office hours are so helpful.

TASK 17

Listen to DVD 1, Clip 6, and consider the ingenious strategy used by a student from Vietnam, named Nam, to overcome his fears. What was his strategy? Could you try this? Do you have other concerns regarding office hours besides language barriers? Discuss these with a partner. Are your concerns shared?

_____

_____

_____

TASK 18

What could you do to prepare for an office hour interaction? Write some strategies in the space below.

_____

_____

_____

UNIT 2

Characteristics of Spoken English and Strategies for Coping

Goals for Unit 2

In this unit you will:

- think about how written English and spoken English are different
- learn about features of naturally occurring speech
- realize the importance of listening to whole pieces of discourse, not just individual words
- learn to listen for word stress and redundancy
- learn strategies for dealing with unfamiliar terms
- learn the importance of background information
- learn to listen for headings and subheadings
- learn to predict before and during lectures
- look at variations in lecture introductions and how introductions can help you
- learn to use summary statements to check your comprehension
- practice note-taking skills such as accuracy, organizing, and abbreviating

Another intended outcome:

- you will gain confidence that good listening skills are achievable

Lectures vs. Textbooks

You have probably thought of English as one single language, but it might be helpful for you to think of English as being one language that has two "codes," one that is written and one that is spoken (Joan Morley, personal communication). That is to say that the English that you read is very different from the English you hear. To understand the differences between these two codes, you will first compare some aspects of language used in textbooks to language used in lectures.

TASK 1

Which of the following features are generally present in a textbook? (Check all that apply.)

_____   several layers of clear organizational structure (units, chapters, section headings)

_____   bolded or italicized new terms

_____   pictures/graphs/tables to illustrate concepts

_____   glossary/index

_____   objective presentation of material

_____   repetition of the main ideas

_____   grammatically correct sentences

_____   typical sentence length (20–30 words)

Since you are already familiar with the organization and language presented in textbooks, you already have strategies for finding and highlighting important information or new information in textbooks. Perhaps you write your own comments or questions in the margins of the text. If you do this, you are using strategies to help you read critically, to make connections to what you already know and react thoughtfully with the material. This is learning!

To help you use more effective strategies when you listen, you will consider some of the language features of a lecture. You may have noticed that the transcript of the BIO 152 (Clip 3) lecture revealed some features of spoken language that you may not have seen before, such as sentences without subjects like "Capable of reproducing?" (Line 14) and informal phrases like "a bunch of properties" (Line 21). We generally don't write down exactly what people say, so reading a transcript can reveal some interesting features of spoken language. Let's have a look at a few more.

TASK 2

STEP 1

Find a few examples of each of the following from the BIO 152 transcript segment and underline them.

- **repetition** of key ideas
- **fillers:** *okay, all right, um, well, uh*
- the **location of the fillers** (at the beginning, middle, or end of a sentence)
- **informal terms** and **slang**
- **reductions:** *gonna*
- **contractions:** *should've*
- **incomplete sentences,** ungrammatical phrases
- **use of personal pronouns:** *I, you, we*

MICASE BIO152 First Day of Class

1 Professor: um, I'll move on. All right?... um, **biology**, simple **definition here**, is just

2 the **study** of **life**. So, that, **begs** the **question**... what is **alive**?... okay who's **gonna give**

3 **me** a **definition** of **what's alive**?

4 Student 1: **things** that, **react** and **reproduce**

5 Professor: **react**, and **reproduce**. Do you have a **grandmother**?

6 Student 1: Yeah

7 Professor: Is she **reproducing**?

8 Student 1: **Not lately**.

9 Professor: Is **she alive**?

10 Student 1: Yeah

11 Professor: So **your definition doesn't work**. So **she's dead** she's you you're

12 **happy** to **redefine** her as **dead**?

13 Student 1: uh... maybe I **should've said** the **possibility** of **reproducing**

14 Professor: **Capable** of **reproducing**? At **some point** in her **life cycle**?

15 Student 1: Right

16 Professor: I **mean** the **same goes true** for **priests** and **nuns** and, and **capable** of

17 **reproducing**... at **some point**. **What** do you **mean by react**, or **somebody else** what

18 does he **mean** by **react**? **Poke** her with a **stick** and she **yells** at you?... **has** to be **able**

19 to **respond**, to, **environment**. Okay. **What** are **other properties** I **mean** what it's

20 **coming down** to is we're gonna, **not really have one easy definition** of **alive** and **not**

21 **alive**. What we're gonna **end up doing** is just, **coming up** with a **bunch** of **properties**

22 of **living organisms**.

23 So **what** are **other properties** of **living organisms**? I know you were **all made** to

24 **memorize this** in **seventh grade**.

25 Student 2:   **consume energy**

26 Professor: **consume energy**. Okay... **who else**?

27 Student 3: **made** of **cells**.

28 Professor: **made** of **cells**? **Made** of **cells**, okay... **that's** at **least true**, for **everything**

29 **we know** on **this planet**, that there **living creatures** are uh, **made** of **cells**... alright..

30 **See** what **I've got** on **my list**... **I've got**... well I I'll just **give you my list** and and

31 we'll **see, how much** that **overlaps metabolism**... uh... **I've got growth** and

32 **reproduction**... so, **growth** in **size and growth** in **number**... and **then I've got**

33 **evolution**... and, **adaptation**. Okay? So, **adaptation** is **basically**, **responding** to your

34 **environment**. **Metabolism** is, **all** the **reactions** that **you do** to, **gather energy** from

35 the **environment** and **convert** it, **into**, uh, **useful, compounds**. um... **Made** of **cells**

36 **like I said** is **how life is** on **this, planet** it's sort of a **consequence** of what's **happened**

37 in **evolution,** here. and **reproduction** we've also **got covered**. Okay?

38 **my** *sort of* a **semi-solid definition** of **life, would be**... anything, that can **convert**

39 **materials**... **from its environment**... **into, more copies of itself**.... okay? So **you have**

40 to be **able** to **take those things, those sugars those chemicals those, buildi- those**

41 **ions those building blocks** that are **out there**, and **convert them** that's the

42 **metabolism part**, into **more copies** of **itself**. So, it it **makes more of itself** and

43 **increases in number**, um, the **fact,** well, I- **living organisms have to be** able to

44 **respond** to their **environment** to **either move away** from **bad things** or **move**

45 **towards**, uh, t- t- to **be able** to **find more** and **collect more materials from** its

46 **environment**. And it's **also** an **inevitable consequence** that in **making copies** of

47 **themselves**, they **don't make perfect copies, therefore** the **subsequent generations**

48 **change** and there's **evolution**.

49 Student 4: Would you say that **has** to **be**, a **natural, occurrence**? I **mean** wh- **when**

50 **you say convert** it **makes me think** of **cloning. We've,** you know, **we've talked**

51 **about science** as um **taking materials** and **making copies** of its um **ourselves**.

52 Professor: Okay, or **cloning would be reproducing**, I- in a **sense** it's **asexual**

53 **reproduction,** but, **even cloning would not work** if the **cell could not carry out**

54 **metabolism**, to **make** the **proteins** that that **second cell** or that **second organism**

55 **needs**, the the **membranes** the **ribosomes** the **D-N-A** the **R-N-A.** So, **cloning does**

56 **require**, um **metabolism** and **growth** in **size before** you can **split** into **two cells** or

57 **two organisms**, which would be than **asexual reproduction.** So, **cloning does fit**

58 **under** sort of, **creation** of **new life**.

59 Y- **you** can **think** of **lots** of **things** like the **classic example is: Is a virus alive**? And

60 **my opinion** is **no** it's **not, because** it **cannot metabolize unless it infects** a **cell** and

61 **convinces** the **cell** to do the **metabolizing for it**. But **things like apple seeds** which,

62 **remain dormant** and **essentially**, are **doing very little** if **any metabolism. Are they**

63 **alive**? *Well, I guess we would say yes* **because** they're **capable** of **metabolism** and

64 **capable** of **growth and reproduction under** the **right conditions**.

65 Student 5: **What about** like a **person in a coma? person** in a **coma** is, **still**

66 **metabolizing**, and, um **they can't do anything** with the **environment** um,

67 Professor: **That's, correct** and **now we're getting into** sort of **sticky philosophical**

68 and **legal definitions**....

Source: R. C. Simpson, S. L. Briggs, J. Ovens, and J. M. Swales. *The Michigan Corpus of Academic Spoken English.* Ann Arbor: The Regents of the University of Michigan, 1999.

STEP 2

Is there anything else you notice about the language used in this portion of the interactive lecture? Are any of these features different from your expectations of spoken English? How are these features different from written English, as you would find in a textbook, for example? Discuss your answers with a classmate.

Hedging

One additional feature we should notice in this passage is some **hedging,** or qualifying language, used in the development of the definition. In Line 38 of the lecture, the professor said: *My sort of, semi-solid definition of life, would be. . . .* How does this differ from: *The definition of life is…?* What is the professor implying? The addition of words like *sort of* can make a difference in how we should view the material. *Sort of semi-solid* is what we call a hedge. The professor is communicating that he is still building the definition and is not yet finished with it. Notice also the phrase (Line 63), *Well, I guess we would say yes.* How is that different from just *yes?* The words *well, I guess,* and the modal *would* all convey a softening and distancing from a straightforward *yes.* In these two examples, the speaker shows some hesitation and a lack of being fully committed. Hedging will be discussed in greater detail in Unit 3.

TASK 3

Now using the BIO 152 transcript and your knowledge of textbooks, fill in the missing information in the chart:

Comparing and Contrasting Written Texts and Lectures

	Textbooks	**Lectures**
Organization pattern	*fairly consistent across disciplines* (units, chapters, sections)	*varies according to field, lecture to lecture, and sometimes even within a single lecture*
How emphasis is shown	*bolded or italicized type*	*repetition; direct statements of "this is my point," "you need to know this because"; volume change*
Predictability/ consistency		
Formality/informality		
Length of sentences		
Grammar		

Discuss which of the aspects of lecture discourse are most challenging for you.

Real Spoken Language Is Real Messy

Now let's look at some of the reasons that the spoken code can be such a challenge. You have begun to see some ways that the English used in a lecture differs from written English. You may have also noticed that the English spoken by the people around you is somewhat different from the English you studied in class. One reason for this is that the language presented in many ESL textbooks, including many listening materials, has not been modeled after naturally occurring speech. It has been common to present formal, unrealistically slow, idealized dialogues in many instructional materials. If you studied from materials that presented English in this kind of idealized manner, then you will be surprised when you encounter naturally occurring speech.

The language teaching methods you may have experienced before now have also unintentionally contributed to your difficulties in comprehending naturally occurring spoken English. For example, if you did not have access to native English speakers as instructors, you will have less familiarity with the sounds of English spoken by native speakers. In addition, you may have had assignments that required you to translate texts. This practice encourages the processing of language word by word. Having to translate texts word by word creates the idea that all words are equal and that processing the parts is as important as processing the whole. This is not true in listening. In spoken English some words are given more emphasis than others because they carry more information. Some words are not spoken at all, as we will soon see.

Finally, if you have watched movies or TV programs in English to help improve your listening comprehension, then you have practiced a good strategy, but the language on TV and movies is scripted and is not exactly naturally occurring speech either.

Everyday spoken English has many interesting and perhaps surprising features. Some of these features add a kind of "messiness" that makes comprehension challenging, but some features of naturally occurring speech can aid your understanding once you become aware of them. We will now look more closely at several features that can create challenges.

Contractions in Spoken English

You are probably familiar with contractions because they are presented in many grammar texts. You know that native speakers typically contract *do not* to *don't* and *cannot* to *can't*, for example. Or maybe you know that *should have* is often contracted to *should've* in spoken English.

One interesting grammatical feature we find when we listen to naturally occurring speech is the way in which speakers create contractions with the modal *will*, which may differ from what most grammar texts describe. Grammar texts present contractions occurring after subject pronouns, as in *I'll* or *he'll*. *It* is often contracted in spoken language producing *it'll*. However, the modal *will* is also sometimes contracted after other nouns you might not expect. For example, the MICASE corpus contains these examples:

...how many *people'll* want to leave..

my *dollar'll* buy half a pound...

this *one'll* be zero...

Native speakers of English contract frequently and, apparently, also create some extra rules for when contractions can occur. You might have suspected that native speakers of English are not following all of the grammar rules that you learned in school. You are also correct if you notice that they are not following many of the rules described in grammar texts.

In addition to frequent contractions, there are several other features of spoken English that can make comprehension difficult. Listen to an audio recording of naturally occurring speech to help you identify some additional features of spoken English. While this audio clip was not recorded from a lecture situation, it demonstrates for you the degree of "messiness" you will hear in real situations in academic environments.

TASK 4

DVD 1, Clip 7, which is audio only, is a recording of an advising session from the MICASE corpus data. An undergraduate is speaking to an advisor about her academic/career interests in order to try to find appropriate courses to take.

STEP 1

Listen to the sound clip twice.

Can you determine what the student's previous career interest was?

_____

_____

What is the new career interest? Why did it change?

_____

_____

_____

STEP 2

Perhaps you understood most of the main ideas in this interaction. If you did, you were able to listen to key words and not focus on all of the other features that are present that may cause difficulties. If you had trouble, you will now see why. As we look at the transcript, you will begin to get a better idea of how much difference there can be between written English and spoken English. Listen to the sound clip again, and at the same time read the transcript that follows. You will notice that there are many bolded words and that there are some symbols that look like a U under some of the words. For now, try to ignore these (these will be discussed later).

MICASE Advising Session

1 Advisor: so **I see** that you're from **Hartland Michigan** (**yes**) this is, **right** up the **road.**

2 Student: **uh** mhm, like **forty minutes** from **here.**

3 Advisor: **yeah** (mhm) and uh, **you say** that **you're interested** in **prebusiness**

4 **and economics.**

5 Student: **I was I don't think** that **I am anymore.**

6 Advisor: **okay** cuz **you write** a **lot** about **international business.**

7 Student: mhm iwro- I w- **I'm interested** in the um, **international aspect**, (uhuh,

8 uhuh) **more**, of a um, of a, **program** or **whatnot so,** like the **international,**

9 **business** I was **gonna do**, it's a **really**, you know **open field**, you know like all

10 that stuff but **I don't, think** that that's what I **wanna do** anymore so.

11 Advisor: (okay) So what, **what changed** your **mind** and **what has** it been **changed to?**

12 Student: um, I **don't know** if I **wanna** sp- like I **wanna experience** like you know,

13 **cultures** and and the **world** and and (mhm) **everything.** And and **business would** be

14 **get me** th- to **these places,** but I **don't know** if **I wanna spend** all my **time** behind a

15 **desk not really enjoying where I am**, you know, like **having** to **work** with **numbers**

16 all the **time** and like, **not really being out, doing something** a little more **interesting**

17 maybe like **flavorful** in any case. **So, I thought about** um, I **don't know if** I I mean

18 even if I ugh I **just don't think business is** and I **I have lots** of **other interests.** Like

19 **um that are** a little bit more like, **paleontology** or **astronomy** or **(oh) international**

20 **religion or uh not religion international relations,** so, **those things I wanna I**

21 think I'm gonna **concentrate more** on, **I don't think I wanna do** the **business.**

STEP 3

Answer the following questions, and then discuss your answers with a partner in class.

1. What features characterize the advisor's language? Can you find any examples of ungrammatical sentences? Are there any terms you don't know? Are there any contractions? Does the speaker speak clearly overall? Does the speaker speak rapidly?

    _____

    _____

    _____

2. What features characterize the undergraduate's language? Are there any examples of ungrammatical sentences? Are there any terms you don't know? Are there any contractions? Does the speaker speak clearly overall? Does she speak rapidly? What other features of her speech did you notice?

    _____

    _____

    _____

3. Did the English of either speaker look or sound like the English dialogues you used when you were studying English in school? What is the same? What's different?

    _____

    _____

    _____

4. Do any of the people you interact with sound like the advisor or the undergraduate? Describe any similarities either of these speakers has to people you have heard.

_____

_____

_____

False Starts

Notice how many times the undergraduate in this advising session begins a sentence and then appears to be searching for words, so she backtracks and begins again (Lines 12, 17, and 20). She has many **false starts** or places where she begins to speak and then stops and begins again. **False starts** are also a part of naturally occurring speech and can make comprehension difficult. You will encounter false starts in lectures; they are part of the open style discussed in Unit 1. However, in lectures they are less frequent than in personal interactions. One reason for this is that experienced lecturers have a high degree of familiarity with their topics, have probably written and spoken about their topics for many years, and have most likely prepared some of what they are going to say ahead of time. When people talk more casually, the frequency of false starts increases because casual speech is largely unprepared and unrehearsed.

Linking

Another feature of naturally occurring speech is **linking.** As proficient speakers speak English, they connect sounds and slide words together. We call this linking. In French grammar, there are explicit rules that tell the speaker to slide certain sounds together in certain environments. For example, learners of French are taught that _vous allez_ (you come) is pronounced /voozalleh/. If you want to speak like the French, you have to say it this way, sliding the sounds together as if these two words were one word. In English, we connect sounds together as we speak as well, but you will probably not see a rule in a grammar book telling you to do this. Connecting sounds is simply what comes naturally to proficient speakers. Proficient speakers will connect words that end in a vowel sound to the next word that begins in a consonant, and they will also connect words that end in a consonant to words that begin with a vowel sound. Look again at the first line of the advising session.

1 Advisor: so **I see** that you're from **Hartland Michigan/ (yes)** this is, **right** up the **road.**

We can see that the vowel sound /ee/ from *see* is linked to the following /th/ sound becoming <u>seethat</u>, the consonant /s/ from *this* is linked to the following vowel in *is* becoming <u>thisis</u>, the /t/ in *right* is linked to the following vowel in *up* becoming <u>rightup</u>, and the /e/ from *the* is linked to the /r/ in *road* becoming <u>theroad</u>. The whole phrase sounds like this: <u>thisis</u> <u>rightup</u> <u>theroad</u>.

Non-native listeners of English will actually hear a stream of sounds run together, then a pause, and then another stream of sounds that are run together. We speak in phrases and pause between the phrases. For this reason, it may be hard for you to identify individual words. And it is no wonder: Many word boundaries that exist on paper do not exist in spoken English, and this is one feature that makes listening comprehension very challenging.

STEP 4

Look again at the transcript for the advising session. The U-shaped symbols under the lines represent places where the speakers connect sounds or link them together.

Listen again to Clip 7 while you read the transcript, and notice how the sounds are linked together. Listen several times if necessary.

Slang and Fillers

You probably also noticed the presence of some other features that add some "messiness" to the dialogue. We see colloquialisms and also fillers here. **Colloquialisms** are informal expressions, such as *all that stuff* (Lines 9 and 10). **Fillers** are words or sounds that have no real meaning in the place where they are used; they are words that fill up a few seconds, usually while the speaker is thinking about what to say next. The fillers we see here are *uh, um,* and *whatnot.*

Reduction

Reduction is the loss of certain sounds or words in naturally occurring speech.

STEP 5

In Lines 10 and 12 of the advising session transcript (as well as many other places), occurs one of the most common examples of reduction: *wanna.* From the transcript, can you determine what *wanna* means? What sounds have been omitted in this reduction?

TASK 5

More examples of reduction and linking occur in this brief dialogue between John and Ann who are talking in the library. The bolded words are spoken more strongly.

1 John: **Jaheet**yet?

2 Ann: No, **joo**?

Do you have any idea what they are talking about? Look at the rest of the dialogue.

3 John: **Well then,** letsavlunch.

4 Ann: Ok, **Wher**dawannaeet?

5 John: **Howbout Starbucks**?

6 Ann: **Starbucks**? Frlunch? I **wannaeat smthing** with **meat** likka **sandwich**.

7 John: **I know**hacha mean, but**heyav good sandwiches**.

8 Ann: Ok, if**yoosay**so. **Let'sgo**after **I finnish**my **calculus problems**.

Can you understand the topic of the dialogue? If you are still having trouble, here is some help.

Fast Speech	Translation
*Jaheet*yet?	*Did you eat yet?*
No, **joo**?	*No, did you?*

If we wrote like we speak, the words on the left would be closer representations of what we actually say. You can see that in addition to linking, we omit parts of words. We call this **reduction** because certain words and sounds become reduced or shortened. We often reduce prepositions, articles, and pronouns. In this example, notice *Howbout Starbucks?* (line 5) The sound of /a/ in *about* is not present. It has been omitted. We also often omit the /h/ from the pronouns *his, him,* and *her* so that in naturally occurring speech they are reduced to /is/, /im/, and /er/.

I saw 'im at the store yesterday.

Ellipsis

Other elements that proficient speakers sometimes shorten or leave out in naturally occurring speech are helping verbs (notice what happened to *have* [Line 3] and *did* [Lines 1 and 2]) and also major grammatical parts of a sentence like the main subject or main verb. We call this **ellipsis**. Most students are taught that, in English, a sentence must have a subject first, then a verb, and then the object. In fact, speakers regularly violate this rule, and the more casual the context, the more this rule is violated. In the previous dialogue, you saw the question: *Howbout Starbucks?* You may understand this as a question that means: *What do you think about Starbucks?* Yet there is neither a subject nor a verb in this question. In the BIO 152 example (p. 31, Line 65), a student asks: *What about like a person in a coma?* This is an example of ellipsis. Both the subject and the verb are absent. Both are implied: *What is your opinion of a person in a coma?*

Assimilation

In addition to sounds and whole words that are omitted in everyday spoken English, sounds are also blended together in many places. We call the blending of sounds **assimilation**. One example you can see in the dialogue is that the *d + y* in *did you* becomes a /j/ sound: *Jaheetyet?* Another example of assimilation that frequently occurs is when one word ends in /t/ and the next word begins with /y/. In this environment, proficient speakers produce a /ch/ sound. Notice in Line 7 of the dialogue on page 40: *I knowwhacha mean.* This would normally be written: *I know what you mean.* The /t/ in *what* has been blended to the /y/ in *you* creating a /cha/ sound producing *whacha*. Another example appears in Line 1 of the advising session from page 36:

> **We read:** *so I see that you're from Hartland Michigan*

> **We hear:** *So I see thacher from Hartland Michigan*

The last /t/ from *that* blends or melts into the /y/ in *you're* creating the /ch/ sound. So as speakers run words together, in some environments sounds actually become very different from how they are represented on paper in the written code.

TASK 6

For extra practice in becoming familiar with the sounds of naturally spoken English, listen to your instructor ask you some questions. Choose the most appropriate response for each question from the choices listed a–h. For example, if you hear, "Howja gethatanswer?" you would select responses c. and d. because they are both approprieate responses. You may use the same answer more than once. Some questions may have two appropriate responses.

1. _____   a. Don't worry, wekinwait.
2. _____   b. Downthehall tuhtheleft.
3. _____   c. Idunno.
4. _____   d. Lemmeshowya.
5. _____   e. Iavamap.
6. _____   f. Iguesso.
7. _____   g. soccer
8. _____   h. The storeonthecorner.
9. _____
10. _____

All Words Are Not Equal

Listening to Stressed Words

You may have begun to think that it will be impossible to ever understand spoken English. But in fact there are some features of naturally occurring speech that can aid your understanding if you can learn to notice these features and use them to your advantage.

One of the most important aspects of learning to understand spoken English is learning to focus on the words that are **stressed**—the words that are spoken more loudly. These stressed words are louder and longer and are spoken at a slightly higher **pitch.** Usually nouns, verbs, major adjectives, and adverbs are stressed—these words carry the most important information. If you can manage to focus on these words, you can get a basic understanding of what you hear, at least enough to understand the main idea. But if you try to listen to every word and have a microscopic view of listening, you will miss both the main idea and the details.

TASK 7

To get an idea of how word stress works, listen again to a short segment from the Rosenthal lecture, DVD 1, Clip 8. Read the transcript as you listen. The bolded words are the ones that she stressed. Listen at least three times. The / represents short pauses. The // represents a longer pause.

Rosenthal Lecture Excerpt

1 in **order** to **talk about** the **American healthcare system**, /which I'd **like** to do

2 this **afternoon,** we **have** to **say** a **few words about America**. // Uh, **like every other**

3 **healthcare system** in the **world**, / our **healthcare system reflects three**

4 **things**. / It **reflects** our **cultural history** and **values**, /ok? Uh it **reflects** our **political**

5 **system** / **and** it **reflects** our **economic philosophy**. / And I would **say** we could **talk**

6 **about any** of the **healthcare systems** of **your countries** /and **we would find** the **same**

7 **thing** to be **true**. / And of course it's **not only true** about the **healthcare system, but**

8 it's **true about every social institution,** / uh **religion,** / **education,** / uh / all the, **family**

9 **structure**/...**all of these things** are a **reflection of those three characteristics**. So

10 **that's very true** of the **American healthcare system** as **well**. //

Proficient speakers stress content words and reduce or do not pronounce as loudly the articles, prepositions, and conjunctions. The words in the previous transcript that are reduced are the ones not bolded. You may have noticed that Professor Rosenthal stresses many words in this passage. You may have also noticed that she stresses content words as well as the preposition *about*. Many speakers would not stress *about* in the way that she does. In fact, it is a little odd that she does this. But one reason that Professor Rosenthal is easier for you to understand than some other speakers is that she stresses so many words. Generally speaking, as words are stressed, they are also slightly lengthened and spoken a little more slowly. As words are reduced, they are slightly shortened and spoken a little more rapidly. This pattern of stressing and not stressing words together with pauses creates the rhythm pattern of the English language.

Proficient speakers of English speak in phrases stressing a couple of words in each phrase and then pausing slightly. Listen again to Clip 8, and read the transcript as you listen. You should begin to hear that the speaker pauses to get a breath. The sounds of English you hear have a rhythm: A group of words are spoken in a phrase with some of them stressed, and then there is a pause and then another group of words are spoken, with some words stressed, and then there is another pause. Using your knowledge of this rhythm pattern and beginning to listen to stressed words in phrases can help you understand spoken English better.

TASK 8

To better understand the pattern of stress, pausing, and reduction of words, read the transcript out loud to a partner and practice making the bolded words louder and hold them <u>slightly</u> longer. Make the non-bolded words softer, and say them <u>slightly</u> more quickly. Pause slightly where the pauses are indicated. Do this several times, and take turns.

TASK 9

Listen again to Clip 7, the advising session. This time, focus on the words that are spoken more loudly. Listen as you read through the transcript again. The bolded words are the ones that are spoken more loudly. Can you identify the telegraphic message given in the louder words? A **telegraphic message** is one that has only the main content words included; it does not contain helping verbs, prepositions, articles, or other grammatical elements.

> **I see....Hartland Michigan... right... road.**

If you can focus on the stressed words, ignore all of the false starts and fillers *(um, uh)*, and become accustomed to certain common reductions *(wanna, gonna)* and blending of sounds, you will have a better chance of understanding the main idea.

You may also have noticed that Professor Rosenthal tends to speak in rather long phrases, and that in the advising session, the undergraduate speaks in very short phrases. Speakers who have planned what they will say or who are very familiar with the topic they are speaking about (e.g., Professor Rosenthal) are more likely to speak in longer phrases.

TASK 10

If you want more practice listening to stressed words, listen again to the MICASE BIO 152 (DVD 1, Clip 3) and review the transcript (p. 29). The bolded words are those he stressed.

Making Use of Redundancy

Another feature of naturally occurring speech that you can use as an aid to comprehension is **redundancy.** In lectures key points are often repeated or rephrased so that the listener can have a second or third opportunity to absorb the information. As a listener, you should take advantage of redundancy. If you feel you don't understand the main point in part of a lecture, keep listening because often the speaker will repeat the same point immediately in a paraphrase or as a summarizing or concluding remark before going on to another topic. You may recall from Professor Rosenthal's lecture that she often repeated important concepts.

TASK 11

Listen to the lecture (DVD 1, Clip 1, at about 2:14) where she was especially redundant with regard to the point about diversity. Read the transcript as you listen.

Now, I think the first thing when we talk about basic, other basic American characteristics is to recognize diversity. America is a very diverse and heterogeneous country. Many of you come from countries where the population shares a very common history for many, many hundreds of years. That is not true in the United States. We are a land of immigrants, so our background is very diverse. And that means many of our institutions are diverse. So the first thing I wanna say about the American healthcare system, is that it is very diverse. So if you said to me: "Choose one word that captures the essence of the American healthcare system." I would have to say diverse, or another word might be heterogeneous. That's a kind of a nice word to add to your vocabulary. But what it means is, there isn't any one system or any one characteristic that describes this whole healthcare system. So the first thing we wanna remember is that it's very diverse in its characteristics.

Most speakers are not this redundant, but you should recognize in this example the importance of listening broadly (not word-by word or translating). You might have had a problem spelling *heterogeneous,* and you may have gotten stuck on it, but you probably still understood the importance of diversity because she was so redundant.

Redundancy in English is a feature that can help you, if you pay attention to it. Try to relax if you don't understand something at first, and keep listening.

Evaluating New Terms

You will always encounter terms that are new for you in lectures. As you notice from this exercise, sometimes speakers will define a term for you immediately as they use the new term. Therefore, if you tend to get stuck on new words, continue to listen for the definition. Two other strategies you can use to make sure you don't get stuck and are able to continue listening are:

- Guess at how the new term is spelled, or at least the first few letters, and write those down. Then, listen for what is said next.
- Write the first letter of the new term with a capital letter, continue listening, and return to the term after the lecture.

For more help understanding definitions and other strategies for dealing with new terms see Unit 3, p. 89.

The Whole Is Greater than the Parts

Several important features of spoken English that affect your listening comprehension have been discussed in this unit. You may be thinking that it is no longer a mystery why the people around you are so difficult to understand. Naturally occurring spoken English is very different from the English that you typically read in a book. In addition, spoken English may have significant differences from the English in the grammar books you studied from and it may be not at all like what you have been exposed to even in prior listening classes.

You can also probably see another reason why translating and processing what you hear using a word-by-word method will be nearly impossible. Many word boundaries are not distinct in spoken English. False starts, colloquialisms, and reductions often occur, all making it very difficult to translate, especially when information is delivered rapidly in a lecture.

Summary of Important Features of Spoken English

Features Causing Difficulties	Aids to Comprehension
• contractions	• word-level stress
• false starts	• pauses
• linking and assimilation	• reduncancy
• colloquialisms and slang	
• reduction	
• ellipsis	
• spoken/written grammar differ	
• unfamiliar terms	

Although the list of features that can cause difficulties is longer than the list of features you can use to aid your comprehension, don't despair! This list of aids to comprehension is still under construction.

Now that you have a better understanding of naturally occurring speech, you will need to adopt some strategies to overcome some of the challenging features of spoken English. Unit 2 will offer more ideas about how to increase your comprehension and provide practice with strategies to help you understand the main ideas in lectures.

The Importance of Background

Students sometimes assume that they can enter a lecture hall with no prior background information about the lecture topic and that they should be able to understand it. Perhaps the most important step to improving your listening comprehension, however, comes *before* the lecture. Before each lecture, consider what the lecturer talked about in the previous class period, and do your best to review the reading materials for the next lecture. You greatly improve your chances to comprehend the lecture material by using as many before class strategies as possible prior to the lecture (review p. 8). In fact, the more background information you have for any listening situation, the more you will understand.

If you do not have time to read the assigned material thoroughly, spend at least a few minutes scanning it. Look at the headings in the text, note some new words (they may be boldfaced), and think about the material. Focus on summaries or conclusions. Even this small amount of preparation will help improve your comprehension. Chances are, your reading skills in English are better than your listening skills in English.

Getting a feel for the topic is important because understanding what you are hearing is not just a matter of taking in words and concepts. Lecture comprehension is a very complex process that requires you to do several things at once, and you must react quickly. To cope with these challenges, you should recall what you already know about the subject of the lecture and try to link what is said to what you already know. In this way, you are activating your brain to be ready to receive the incoming information; you are thinking about what you already know, applying it to what you hear, and beginning to interpret the new information.

> Previous knowledge + understanding what you are hearing = interpretation of new information

In Clip 9, you will hear from a student about the lecture preparation strategies that she finds most useful.

TASK 12

STEP 1

Watch DVD 1, Clip 9. Xiaoyu, a student, will tell you about the preparation strategies she uses to help her to follow a lecture. What does she do?

_____

STEP 2

How often do you use these strategies?

_____

_____

_____

STEP 3

Many students find that spending massive amounts of time reading the course material after the lecture can help them compensate for what they missed during the lecture. However, this may not be the best strategy. Can you think of one reason why this might be true?

_____

_____

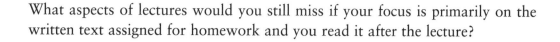

What aspects of lectures would you still miss if your focus is primarily on the written text assigned for homework and you read it after the lecture?

Big Picture Listening: Listening for and Recording Headings

When you are listening you should try to get the main idea because that will anchor you to the details, which will make understanding the whole lecture possible. Often a speaker will tell you the main idea and then develop it with details. If you only listen narrowly to individual words that you then translate, you may miss the comments the speaker gives about the main ideas. While statements indicating a main idea can come at any point in the lecture, they most often come at the beginning of a section.

Since professors in the United States tend to lecture in an open style, they also generally recognize the need to create an obvious organizational structure to reinforce the main ideas. To organize their talks, lecturers make announcements of what they intend to do and sometimes they tell you why they intend to do it.

Lecturers may use phrases like these:

- *Today I'm going to talk about X because.* . . .
- *First I want to talk about.* . . .
- *So, let's get on with today's topic.*
- *I'm gonna try to illustrate three reasons for.* . . .
- *So why is this important?*
- *Ok, next I wanna talk about.* . . .
- *Let's move on to the other aspect.*

> If you can try to listen for comments like these, you will be more able to "see the forest for the trees." That is, you will not be so focused on the individual trees (words) that you miss the forest (the main point).

In a written text, you find headings like the one above: *Big Picture Listening: Listening for and Recording Headings.* These organizational markers orient readers and help them anticipate what is coming next in a written text. In the same way, lecturers typically use statements that we could also call headings or announcements of what is coming next. In addition to the headings that provide general orientation, lecturers use subheadings that explain the purpose of the examples or details being presented.

We would like all speakers to be like Professor Rosenthal, outlining the material on the board, speaking slowly, announcing the topics clearly (giving headings), and being redundant, but most lecturers do not give all these comprehension clues to the listeners. Most lecturers do give some clues, though. Your job is to understand what these clues are and **to make sure that you write headings in your notes** so that you can follow the main ideas and know how the examples are linked to the main ideas.

In the BIO 152 definition, the first heading (Line 1) is:

biology, //simple definition here,/ is just the study of life //.

The speaker was introducing this section of the lecture with a statement after which he proceeded to give the definition. Listen again to the very beginning of Clip 3. Notice also the higher pitch and louder volume on the first word *biology*. A pitch rise like this with pauses can be a signal of a new topic.

In Professor Rosenthal's lecture there was a clear heading before each section of the lecture to orient the audience. Here is the first one from Clip 1:

In order to talk about the American healthcare system
which I'd like to do this afternoon
we have to say a few words about America.

Replay this short piece again, the very beginning of Clip 1, and listen for the intonation pattern. There is relatively high pitch on this introductory heading. It is then followed by a pause, and the following statements each take a slightly lower pitch as she continues talking. A new topic is often announced with a slightly higher pitch and also a pause before and after the statement.

You will now have a chance to identify headings in a lecture. You will focus on the clues that the speaker gives to help orient his listeners—statements that indicate what he intends to talk about and why and the statements that connect things together. He gives both major headings to orient his listeners and minor headings or subheadings to explain the purpose of his examples.

TASK 13

STEP 1

Watch DVD 1, Clip 10. The title of this lecture was "English in Today's Research World." For our purposes here, we will listen only to the first portion about the history of English. Professor Swales will briefly discuss the two major languages that were combined and led to modern English. As a preparation strategy, think about which languages these might be. Do you know what important historical event brought this linguistic mixing about? Discuss your ideas with a partner. Write some of your ideas here.

_____

_____

_____

STEP 2

Listen to Clip 10 once, and take notes. Try to listen for headings like the ones on page 49, remembering that a rise in pitch and a longer pause may signal the heading. Write your notes in the space.

_____

_____

_____

_____

_____

_____

STEP 3

Analyze your notes. Listen again, and focus on the headings. Did you write only the material that Professor Swales wrote on the board? Did you note any headings he gave? Listen a second time, and focus again on the headings. Add them to your notes using a different colored pen if you missed them the first time. The first headings he gave provided important information regarding a main point. Professor Swales uses fairly dramatic intonation variation and longer and more frequent pauses than some other lecturers. He tends to write only the details on the board.

STEP 4

Have a look at the beginning part of the lecture. The first few headings are identified for you below.

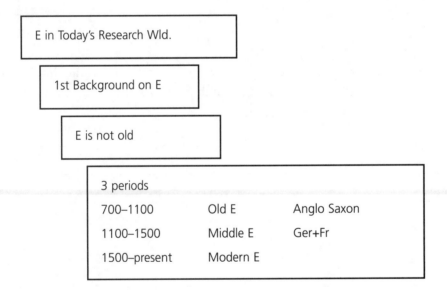

E in Today's Research Wld.

1st Background on E

E is not old

3 periods

700–1100	Old E	Anglo Saxon
1100–1500	Middle E	Ger+Fr
1500–present	Modern E	

STEP 5

Now listen again to Clip 10. Professor Swales wrote some details about farm animals, though not the headings, on the board. You probably copied the details of the animals and the names of the meats, but did you also write the subheadings or the comments about what they were illustrating in your notes? You should have. This is important information that helps to orient you to the topic. Often this shows the links between the details and the rest of the lecture. Most students will naturally copy the material the instructor writes on the board, but many will miss the orienting statements or headings that the instructor gives or will fail to put that information in their notes for later reference. Here is the important information from this portion of the lecture.

1100–1500: ME

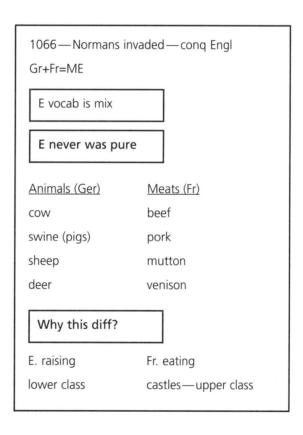

1066 — Normans invaded — conq Engl

Gr+Fr=ME

E vocab is mix

E never was pure

Animals (Ger)	Meats (Fr)
cow	beef
swine (pigs)	pork
sheep	mutton
deer	venison

Why this diff?

E. raising   Fr. eating

lower class   castles — upper class

Notice the subheading at the end of this example: *Why this difference?* It takes the form of a rhetorical question. **A rhetorical question** is a thought-provoking question that the speaker uses; the speaker does not intend for students to answer it. Rhetorical questions are often used as organizational markers, as transitions or to signal important points. Such organizational devices are also used by lecturers to add a bit of variation to their presentations and to make students think. Sometimes rhetorical questions are answered immediately by the lecturer, as in the example here, but sometimes the question may be answered much later in the lecture or maybe not at all. Maybe you will have to answer one later on a test.

TASK 14

You will now listen to the next portion of the same Swales lecture. Watch DVD 1, Clip 11. Take notes. Listen twice if you need to. Compare your notes to the sample notes in Appendix C (pp. 147–48).

What are the important new headings and subheadings in this section? Discuss your ideas with a partner. Are any of these written on the board?

_____

_____

_____

_____

_____

For help getting oriented to the bigger picture, from now on, try to listen for headings, which are often signaled by

- a specific transition statement
- louder volume
- a rise in pitch
- a longer pause
- a rhetorical question

Predicting Before and During Lectures

Increasing your background knowledge and listening for headings will improve your comprehension. Predicting or **guessing what will come next** is another important strategy to use when listening to a lecture. Keeping your mind active while you listen will keep you focused (and help to keep you from daydreaming). Listening is not a passive event that happens to you. It's important to be constantly evaluating the incoming information in light of what you already know and thinking about where the lecturer may be going and what the larger point may be. Have you noticed that before you listen to each clip in this textbook that you are asked to think about what you already know about the topic? This is reinforcing the significance of this step in preparing to listen.

As you apply the strategy of predicting, you will probably guess incorrectly at times, and this could cause temporary problems. But guessing will aid your comprehension. Of course, you cannot guess very intelligently if you don't have any background—so these two strategies work best if you apply both of them. At least skim the readings ahead of time, and prepare a list of questions you have or prepare a list of topics you think will be covered. Then, as you listen to the lecture, constantly refine your guesses as new information is given.

TASK 15

You will now apply the strategies of getting background material and predicting to a lecture. The title of the next lecture is "An Introduction to Agroecology" by Ricardo Carvajal (DVD 1, Clip 12). At the time of this lecture, Carvajal was a Ph.D. student in the Department of Biology at the University of Michigan.

STEP 1

Carvajal instructed his audience to do an Internet search for the terms *sun coffee* and *shade coffee* before listening to his lecture. You should do this, too. Write a brief definition for each term in the following space. Then think about issues the field of agroecology might address, and make some predictions about the lecture content. Discuss your information from the Internet search and your ideas about the content with a partner.

_____

_____

_____

_____

_____

STEP 2

Listen to the introduction of the lecture (Clip 12 to about the first 12 minutes) and take notes. (Please note: Early in the lecture [after about 2 minutes] a student answers a question. You cannot hear the student's answer, but Carvajal repeats it for you. This is often the case—lecturers realize that not everyone can hear student questions and comments so they sometimes repeat them or paraphrase them.) After you listen to this section, revise your predictions from Step 1. Do you now think anything different will be covered in the lecture? Why? Describe the mismatch between what you had prepared and what he has talked about so far.

_____

_____

_____

_____

_____

_____

_____

_____

_____

_____

_____

STEP 3

Listen to the rest of lecture and take notes.

STEP 4

Discuss your answers to the following with a partner.

1. In what ways was it useful to have background knowledge and make predictions before and during this lecture? Which part of the lecture was easiest for you?

_____

_____

_____

2. What are the possible limitations for preparing for and guessing the content of a lecture? Might the benefits outweigh the limitations?

_____

_____

_____

STEP 5

1. Look at the sample notes for the first section of the introduction to agro-ecology lecture (Appendix C, pp. 148–49). In what ways are your notes different from or similar to the sample notes?

Consider:

- use of abbreviations and symbols
- use of headings
- indentation
- highlighted information (circled, etc.)
- use of white space (empty space on the page vs. writing)
- completeness
- readability

Is there any important information missing from your notes? If yes, what? Why do you think you missed it?

STEP 6

1. Explain how you dealt with the primary visual (picture of the coffee growing systems). How did having background on this subject influence your note taking on this part of the lecture? Did you copy the picture only? Did you write the commentary? Which do you think was the most important to record?

_____

_____

_____

_____

_____

Taking Advantage of Lecture Introductions

Lecturers give introductions to help the listeners prepare for the information that will be presented. They expect that their introduction will help orient their listeners to the material and improve their understanding of it. In addition to using the strategies for getting background information and predicting, you should always use whatever the lecturer provides in terms of an introduction to be more prepared for the lecture. Sometimes in the first few minutes of class, instructors deal with various administrative details (questions about the assignments or upcoming exams), which precede the actual lecture introduction. You will want to be ready for any information given at the beginning of class because it could be important for you, both for your lecture comprehension and for general knowlege of what is going on.

TASK 16

1. Consider the introduction to the agroecology lecture. Which of the following best describe this introduction?
   - Outline of material that will be covered
   - Important background information
   - Extended example
   - Other

   Why do you think the lecture began this way?

   _____

   _____

2. Carvajal gave a heading before he gave the example of the zebra mussels. He says, "Now in order to give you an idea how complicated this can get, I'll give you an example that's important here in Michigan." Did you write that heading in your notes to help orient yourself to the example?

TASK 17

Analyze Carvajal's lecture. Discuss and answer the following questions with a partner.

1. What do you think the main purpose (main point) of the lecture was? At what point in the *introduction* was the theme introduced (beginning, middle, end)? How was this idea reinforced in the rest of the lecture? Did you record this theme in your notes and highlight it?

_____

_____

_____

_____

2. This was a stand-alone lecture (i.e., informational, not part of a class that met regularly). How does this introduction compare to those you have encountered in other lectures that meet weekly, if you have experienced regularly meeting lectures?

_____

_____

_____

_____

_____

_____

The introduction to the agroecology lecture began with some general background about the field and an extended local example. This kind of lecture introduction may be common, but introductions vary in terms of content. We will now take a look at some of this variation.

TASK 18

Think more about the classes you have attended in the past. What information is typically given in the first few minutes of a class or a lecture? Look at the following list, and check all the features that you typically encounter in the first few minutes of class in the **lefthand column.** Discuss your list with a partner. (In the following exercise, listen to the first few minutes of a lecture on addictive drugs and compare it to the first few minutes of classes you typically encounter.)

Typical Lecture	Addictive Drug Lecture
_____	_____ administrative tasks (handouts, announcements)
_____	_____ information about exams
_____	_____ references to your reading material
_____	_____ relating lecture material to other events
_____	_____ indicating the importance of this information
_____	_____ indicating the scope and depth of today's lecture
_____	_____ joking
_____	_____ giving questions to think about during the lecture
_____	_____ information about future lectures
_____	_____ summary of previous lecture
_____	_____ definitions of key terms
_____	_____ outline of the main points
_____	_____ invitations for interaction

As you compared your list on the left to your classmate's list, you probably noticed that there is some variation of what can take place in the first few minutes of class.

TASK 19

STEP 1

Listen to the first few minutes of a lecture on addictive drugs from the MICASE files (DVD 1, Clip 13). This example is audio only. Before you listen, as a preparation strategy, study some terms you will encounter. Look up the syllable stress and the definition for each.

hypnotics   sedatives   hallucinogens   opiates

_____

_____

_____

_____

STEP 2

Listen to Clip13, and focus on the features from the list on page 60 that may be found in the first few minutes of a class. Check any elements that you hear in the **righthand column** of the chart on page 60.

STEP 3

In this audio clip, you heard some basic information about the exam schedule and what will be covered in the next few classes. Listen again to Clip 13, and take notes on what you think is important for a student in that class to record. Compare them with a classmate. Did both of you write the necessary information? Did you use any abbreviations?

_____

_____

_____

STEP 4

Examine the transcript for this lecture to determine which of the five features of the beginning of class you listed on page 60 are present and where they are. First, underline the sentence where you find each feature, and then write in the margin which type of information is given. For example, on Lines 2 and 3 of the transcript, you see that *change in the lecture schedule* has been underlined. In the margin near Line 2, you should write lecture schedule change .

Other things you might write in the margin are:

exam info

future lecture info

The first few have been underlined for you. Compare your findings with a classmate.

MICASE Addictive Drug Lecture Introduction

1 Professor: Okay let's get started... couple of uh, quick announcements. Just to repeat

2 uh, the announcement that I made last... day which concerns a <u>change in the lecture</u>

3 <u>schedule</u> as you see up there. So after the, the exam on Tuesday, that's a reminder that,

4 <u>the next exam is on, this coming Tuesday</u>. uh <u>after that</u> we're going to go on, and <u>uh</u>

5 <u>talk about opiates</u>. So you wanna print out the uh lecture notes for opiates next.

6 there'll be four four, lectures on opiates followed by two, uh periods of addiction and

7 then we'll finish up with sedative hypnotics. Okay? Just, make sure you get that down

8 so you have the right lecture notes when you come. The, again the format for the, next

9 exam, on Tuesday will be exactly the same as the format, for the last exam. Any

10 questions about the lecture schedule, or the exam?

11 Student 1: When is the question and answer session?

12 Professor: Oh right right right. So there will be a question and answer session,

13 Monday, four o'clock, uh on the terrace on the fourth floor of this building. There's a,

14 terrace there. Monday four o'clock, open question and answer session. Anything else?

15 Okay. yup. okay. So today, we're ready to go on, to have the last lecture on

16 hallucinogens. And last day we had talked about the two major families of

17 hallucinogens, the L-S-D family. All of which have a a common structure similar to

18 the neurotransmitter, serotonin. and the phenyl ethylamine family. The prototypical,

19 uh phenyl ethylamine hallucinogen being mescaline. and all of the, phenyl ethylamine

20 family, of hallucinogens has structural similarity to catecholamine neurotransmitters.

21 So what we're gonna talk about today then is what's known about the, neural

22 biological mechanism of action, of the hallucinogens.

<u>STEP 5</u>

At what point does the instructor really begin the introduction to the lecture (which line in the transcript)? What intonation and pausing features signal this? Listen again if you need to. What words signal this?

_____

_____

_____

_____

Notice that the professor discusses the date of the next exam (Line 4), discusses the order and topics for the next few lectures (Lines 4–7), and then returns briefly to the topic of the format of the exam (Lines 8–9). Speakers often partially address a topic, jump to another topic, and return to the initial topic again. This is another feature of naturally occurring speech that can inhibit comprehension. One strategy you can use to help with note taking is to leave plenty of space between topics so that if the speaker returns to a previous topic, you have some space to add information.

TASK 20

Discuss and answer the following questions with a classmate:

- How important is it that you listen to these introductory remarks in a lecture and understand them?

- What strategies would best serve you.to prepare to listen for this information? (Review the before-lecture strategies on p. 8.)

_____

_____

_____

_____

TASK 21

Notice some challenging new terms in the addictive drug introduction (*phenyl ethylamine, mescaline*). What **before-lecture** strategy would help you to prepare for encountering such difficult terms?

TASK 22

How did you respond to the classroom noise that occurred in the addictive drug class as students were settling down? If you were a student in this class and had some difficulty following everything that was said, how could you make sure you got the information you needed? Where might be the best place to sit?

_____

_____

TASK 23

STEP 1

1. You are next going to listen to an introduction to the lecture entitled A Conversation about Global HIV/AIDS by Professor Pollack (DVD 1, Clip 14). Professor Pollack was a faculty member at the University of Michigan School of Public Health when this lecture was recorded. What predictions can you make about what his focus might be, now that you know his position?

    _____

    _____

2. Before you listen, think about what you know already about the global AIDS epidemic. Discuss your ideas with a classmate and write some of your ideas.

    _____

    _____

    _____

<u>STEP 2</u>

Listen to Clip 14, and check which of the following features are present:

_____ administrative details (handouts, exams, homework)

_____ references to the reading material

_____ relating lecture material to world events

_____ indicating the importance of this information

_____ indicating the scope and depth of today's lecture

_____ joking

_____ giving questions to think about during the lecture

_____ information on future lectures

_____ information from previous lectures

_____ definitions of key terms

_____ invitation to interact

<u>STEP 3</u>

Listen to Clip 14 again, and take notes in the space.

_____

_____

_____

_____

<u>STEP 4</u>

Answer the following questions. Then compare your answers with a partner.

1. Why do you think Professor Pollack called his introduction a roadmap?

_____

_____

2. What strategies do you think serve you best for listening to a lecture introduction?

_____

_____

_____

3. What can you do if the professor does NOT give such an outline for you to develop your expectations?

_____

_____

_____

Even though we don't have the opportunity to listen to the rest of Professor Pollack's lecture, it can be predicted that he will follow his roadmap outline. Lecturers may give you a clear roadmap in their introduction, as in this lecture, or they may give you lengthy background in the introduction, as in the example from Professor Rosenthal (Clip 1). Lecturers may give administrative details and briefly list what will be covered in the next few lectures, as in the example from the MICASE lecture on addictive drugs (Clip 13). Sometimes a lecturer may provide a summary of the previous class period. It is also possible that a lecturer will just start talking with no introduction. Your job is to take advantage of whatever is given.

TASK 24

Discuss with a partner which introduction types are most common for classes you have attended in your field of study.

- lengthy background (Rosenthal)
- extended example (Carvajal)
- administrative details, brief summary of last lecture and next few lectures (MICASE)
- road map (overview) (Pollack)
- the speaker just starts talking
- other

The audience and their background will often determine what kind of introduction is given. For example, lengthy background is often given in contexts where the audience may have little previous knowledge, such as, for the first day of a new unit or for conference presentations where the audience may have different backgrounds. If the audience shares less in common, then the speaker needs to give more background. If the audience shares a lot, as in the case when half of the course is already finished, then less background may be provided.

TASK 25

Discuss with a partner the kinds of lecture introduction you have encountered most frequently in the past.

TASK 26

For one lecture in your field, or for a lecture included in this text in the extra practice section, think about the topic that will be covered. Do a little research on the Internet to find out about the lecturer and the topic, and make a list of vocabulary or technical words you predict that you will encounter. Then attend or listen to the lecture and take notes. Use the introduction to help you refine your predictions. Evaluate the effectiveness of these strategies. How much did getting background and predicting aid your comprehension? How useful was the lecture introduction for helping you to understand the whole lecture? Discuss this exercise with a partner.

_____

_____

_____

Using the Summary Statements

Lecturers will sometimes provide a summary of the important points in the lecture. A summary section can occur at the end of one part of a lecture or at the end of the whole lecture, or both, or neither. If a summary is given, you should use this opportunity to check your understanding and fill in any gaps that you may notice.

Summary statements often begin with a filler, the word *so*, and some kind of heading indicating that a summary is coming.

> *Okay, so what I tried to do today...*
> *Alright, so what we've seen here is...*
> *So, what I'm trying to illustrate here is...*

TASK 27

<u>Note</u>: In order to understand this task, students will need to have listened to all of the Rosenthal lecture (DVD 3, Clips 20–22).

For an example of a summary of the main points at the end of a lecture, listen to Professor Rosenthal's final summary (DVD 3, Practice Unit, Clip 22, almost 6 minutes after the beginning of the clip). As you listen, read the following transcript of Professor Rosenthal's final summary. Notice how she signals the beginning of the summary (Line 1). On the transcript, underlined for you are the places where she repeats the main points from the lectures.

Notice how the summary begins. Professor Rosenthal begins with *okay so,* then she pauses and her intonation rises as she says, "What I've tried to do this afternoon. . . ." These are signals also used to indicate a topic change, which will be discussed later.

Professor Rosenthal's Final Summary

1 Okay, so what I've tried to do this afternoon in a very brief summary, is to give you a

2 general introduction to the characteristics of the American health care system and I've

3 alerted you that in order to understand the system you have to understand the country.

4 The system, the <u>health care system in my country is a reflection of the overall values in</u>

5 <u>the political and economic philosophy of our country</u> and the same thing is true of your

6 health care systems. So I've made that connection, I've I've told you about some of the

7 <u>important characteristics of the system</u>. Uh, I've given you a <u>little introduction to what</u>

8 <u>it takes to be educated as a doctor in in the United States,</u> I've told you about our <u>major</u>

9 <u>problems.</u> Uh and I've indicated some of the <u>current debate</u> about health policy in the

10 United States and <u>how it's related to the central issue of how much the government</u>

11 should do and how much the marketplace should do. We are struggling like your

12 countries are struggling to find the right combination, the right balance of government

13 regulation and marketplace dynamics. And uh I've tried to summarize the strengths

14 and the weaknesses of the country. So now I've had my say and now I'd like to hear from you.

TASK 28

Discuss with a classmate what you think would be a good strategy to use after a final summary is given and the lecture has ended. For example, you could:

• stay in your seat and compare the points indicated in the final summary to your notes

• highlight any missing information

• try to write a summary of the lecture in your own words

• ask a classmate to clarify any points that remain unclear

Remember the list of Aids to Comprehension from page 47? That list had three features of spoken English that you can take advantage of to help you get the main idea in any listening situation. We can now add the lecture listening strategies from the latter half of this unit to our list (items in bold) for some additional strategies and items you can use and focus on to help you better understand lectures.

Aids to Comprehension

• word-level stress
• pauses
• redundancy
• **background knowledge**
• **headings**
• **predicting**
• **introductions**
• **summary statements**

TASK 29

This final exercise will help you focus on several of the features of spoken English and strategies for listening that you have learned about in this unit. Listen to a short talk given by Officer Mathews on campus safety (DVD 1, Clip 15). The strategies you should use are *predicting and using background knowledge; listening for headings; and listening to word-level stress, pauses, and redundancy.*

STEP 1

Discuss with a classmate what you can do to learn about campus crime and what you can do to be safe on your campus. Then look up information about campus safety on the Internet. After you find information, discuss the results. Make some predictions about the talk and what you think you will hear.

STEP 2

Listen to DVD 1, Clip 15, and take notes in the space.

_____

_____

_____

_____

STEP 3

Answer these questions:

1. What is the most common crime on campus?

_____

2. How can it be avoided?

_____

3. Describe how this type of crime commonly happens.

_____

4. What items are commonly stolen?

_____

5. What other safety tips are given with regard to serial numbers, ATM machines, and walking at night?

_____

_____

_____

_____

_____

STEP 4

Officer Mathews's talk has some features of an informal talk (an open style). Some of the features of this talk that convey informality are:

- the setting: a small classroom, not a large lecture hall

- conversational style

- slang: *computers are a very hot ticket item to steal; that's a big no no*

- linking and reduction: *it's better to do that than ta hafta try ta borrow notes from somebody; they're gonna probably want some o that money*

- addressing the audience as *you*

STEP 5

Officer Mathews gives some direct advice in this talk. He uses command forms here:

> *Do not leave any of your property unattended for any amount of time.*
> *Secure your property at all times and it means all times.*
> *Make sure that every thing you have that you can't live without is with you at all times.*

Why do you think he is so direct? What is the purpose of this talk?

_____

_____

_____

STEP 6

Notice the redundancy present in Officer Mathews's talk. Why do you think he repeated himself so much?

_____

STEP 7

1. Does the information that Officer Mathews gave surprise you in any way?

    _____

    _____

2. What kinds of crimes are typical on the campuses that you are familiar with?

UNIT 3

Understanding Lecture Organizational Elements and Other Features of Lectures

In this unit you will:

- begin to recognize organizational features in lectures
- begin to identify and show hierarchical relationships in your notes
- learn how new terms are introduced
- learn to recognize some evaluative comments
- consider good ways to handle visual material and commentary on the visuals
- study signals that indicate a change in topic
- understand how formality and informality affect your comprehension
- think about a speaker's purpose
- learn why jokes are so difficult to understand
- learn that digressions may be important
- improve note-taking skills such as abbreviating, accuracy, and organizing

Another intended outcome:

- you'll gain confidence that good listening skills are achievable

In Unit 2 we began to look at how having background information before a lecture will help us understand it better, and we also began to look at how introductions can be used to develop expectations and how summaries can be used to check comprehension. In Unit 3 we will think more about both the larger patterns, or **macro patterns** that lecturers use to organize a lecture, and we will also learn how lecturers organize information more locally into smaller pieces that we will call **micro elements**. Finally, we will look at some additional features of lectures, such as ways lecturers convey opinions, strategies for dealing with visuals, and how a speaker's style may affect your comprehension.

Lecture Organization: Macro Patterns

One significant aid to lecture comprehension is to have a greater awareness of the organization patterns that lecturers use. On occasion, this is directly stated: "Today we're going to talk about the causes and consequences of financial crises in emerging market economies." This kind of macro-structuring comment lets you know how the lecture is organized, and in this case, you can expect an organization pattern that will include causes and effects. Sometimes no direct statement revealing the overall organization pattern is given, and you have to determine the organization based on previous lectures, the content, the reading material, and the introduction. Whatever cues you are given, it is helpful to build a mental model of the overall pattern so that you can make predictions about what is coming next, organize your notes better, and ultimately understand the lecture better.

Recall the exercise we did comparing textbooks to lectures (p. 33). Textbooks have units or chapters as well as subsections, all of which make the organization transparent. Lectures usually have an overall pattern (macro elements) and also a series of shorter patterns (micro elements), but the organization in lectures is not nearly as transparent as it is in textbooks.

Variation across disciplines exists with regard to how lectures are organized and presented. In many engineering fields, for example, lectures may be organized around a problem, its solution, and an evaluation of the solution and may involve many formulas; in dentistry or medicine, the lecture may be focused on a process description and structured around viewing slides. In addition to variation across fields, there is variability within disciplines and even from lecture to lecture by the same instructor. This poses some great challenges for non-native speakers, as well as for students whose native language is English.

Sometimes the larger organization pattern may not be apparent until the lecture is finished and after you had time to think about it and study all the subsections. To help you identify patterns, especially when they are not overtly stated, some common macro patterns are listed here. **Lectures may be a combination of several of these patterns.**

Table 1: Common Macro Lecture Patterns

Lecture Type	Characteristics
Information–driven	The focus is primarily on delivery of information or facts. Topics are followed by explanation and/or a listing of items.
Problem/solution	This pattern is structured around a problem or equation. One or several solutions are proposed, which may result in new problems and possibly new solutions.
Comparative	Two or more competing theories are presented in comparison and/or contrast to each other.
Thesis/point-driven	There is a single (or several) point(s) made, followed by support. Examples are presented to illustrate a main point. Support may be given first, followed by an argument at the end.
Cause and effect	Causes and effects are developed as a set of related events or influences.
Data vs. theory	Theory is examined in light of data, or data is examined with regard to theory.
Sequential	Information or theories are presented in chronological order or in order dictated by a process.
Classification/description	This pattern highlights systems of classification and descriptions of key elements.

TASK 1

If you have listened to all of Professor Rosenthal's lecture (DVD 1, Clip 1; DVD 3, Clips 20–22), discuss with a partner what you think the main organization pattern was. Review your notes if you need to. Was it information-driven? Did she also have a point or a thesis? What do you think the major pattern in the Carvajal lecture was (DVD 1, Clip 12)? If it was point-driven, what was (were) his point(s)? Can you identify any other patterns in Carvajal's lecture?

_____

_____

_____

_____

As a good after-lecture strategy, you should review your notes and reflect on the overall organization patterns(s). This will help you evaluate your understanding of the lecture.

Lecture Organization: Micro Elements

In Unit 2 we considered the several layers of organization patterns present in textbooks. Units, chapters, chapter sections, and paragraphs all represent different layers of organization that writers impose on their texts to make things clear to readers. We have also seen that lectures usually have an overall macro pattern that we may identify, such as problem-solution or thesis-driven. In addition to this overall structure, we can think of lectures as made up of a set of smaller parts that we will call micro elements. For our purposes here, a micro element can be thought of as a relatively short part within a lecture that can be identified as having a unique function. You could think of a micro element as being the spoken equivalent of a paragraph. You could also think of the macro pattern as the house and the micro elements as the rooms that make up the house.

Some common micro elements in lectures are:

- overview/background
- definition/extended definition
- process description
- example/extended example
- comparison/contrast
- analogy
- evaluation or emphasis*
- description
- summary/conclusion

*An evaluation is a judgment about the content.

The organization of a lecture could have various micro elements occurring in various orders, throughout the lecture. A lecture's organization could look like this:

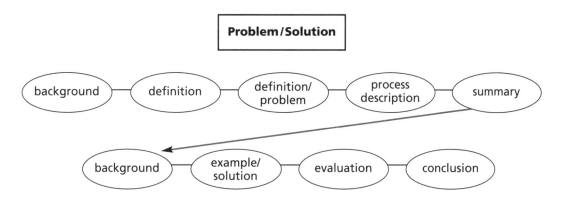

Figure 1: Macro Pattern of Problem/Solution Lecture

Figure 1 shows an overall macro pattern of a problem-solution lecture. Within the problem-solution framework, a lecturer could introduce the micro elements of background information, definitions, process description, summary, and then the lecturer could continue with more background, add an example, evaluate that example, and conclude.

To illustrate some of these micro elements, we will review some subsections from lectures we have listened to previously. You are already familiar with the lecturer's style and the content in these lectures. Now we will focus on the micro elements and how they are signaled. This should help you identify the language clues that often accompany these micro elements.

TASK 2

Table 2 shows four micro sections, one each from Professor Rosenthal's lecture and the BIO 152 class, and two from Ricardo Carvajal's lecture. The table provides the following information: (a) the lecturer, location, and content; (b) the micro element; and (c) the language clues or headings that can help you identify the micro element. Use the fourth column to show how to represent this information in your notes. Return to these lectures for the timeframes indicated in the table (as noted in the parentheses), and listen to these sections again. Notice especially the language cues used to signal the micro elements.

Table 2: Identifying Micro Elements

Lecturer/content of subsection	Micro-organizational pattern	Language clues/ headings	How/whether to record it in your notes?
Rosenthal Cultural values reflected in health-care system (DVD 1, Clip 1) (2:53)	evaluation	"So if you said to me choose one word that captures the essence of the American healthcare system, I would have to say diverse."	diversity capt. essence of h.c.syst.
BIO 152 lecture What it means to be alive (DVD 1, Clip 3) (17:56)	definition by listing properties	"What are other properties? I mean what it's coming down to is we're gonna not really have one easy definition of alive and not alive. What we're gonna end up doing is just coming up with a bunch of properties of living organisms."	
Carvajal Zebra mussels (DVD 1, Clip 12) (20:30)	extended example	"Um, now in order to give you an idea of how complicated this can get, I'll give you an example that's important here in Michigan."	
Carvajal Zebra mussels (DVD 1, Clip 12) (28:04)	reason for example/ main point	"Um, probably the most important consequence of this invasion of zebra mussels has been an overall loss of what we call bio-diversity."	

Usually language clues that signal a micro element occur before the section begins, but sometimes the clues occur toward the end as the speaker is concluding that section. Sometimes clues occur in both places. It is important for you to listen for these clues so that you can identify and predict what is coming next and begin to put the pieces together.

TASK 3

To fill out the final column of Table 2, look again at the sample notes provided for these sections (Appendix C, pp. 148–49). How was this information indicated in the sample notes?

_____

_____

_____

_____

We can think of the language clues in each of these sections as **signposts.** Just as a road sign tells you where you are, these clues tell you what is going on or what has gone on. As noted in Unit 2 on headings, such clues are very important for you to listen for as they will help you find your way in a lecture. They will help you know what the speaker is doing; for example, they will help you know the difference between the examples and the main point. The clues may not always be given, in which case you have to figure out what is going on without them.

In the next lecture, "What's a laser?" you will have an opportunity to focus more on a few micro elements, such as definitions, background, and examples. You should focus first on the content, and then you will have a look at the micro elements.

TASK 4

STEP 1

Listen to the first half of a lecture on laser light (DVD 2, Clip 16). Professor Winful is a Professor of Electrical Engineering and Computer Science at the University of Michigan. He will discuss basic principles in physics that are used to create laser light. Some basic terms you will encounter include _atom, electron,_ and _photon._ Most of the other important terms are defined in the lecture. Before you watch this lecture, do an Internet search to find out what the acronym LASER represents. Write your notes from your Internet search in the space:

_____

_____

_____

_____

STEP 2

Listen to the first 24 minutes of the lecture by Professor Winful titled "What's a laser?" (DVD 2, Clip 16). Take notes on a separate page.

STEP 3

Answer the following comprehension questions from your notes.

1. What does the acronym LASER stand for?

   _____

   _____

2. Describe the "ground state" of an electron.

   _____

   _____

3. Describe the process of "spontaneous emission."

   _____

   _____

4. What is included in the definition of "light"?

   _____

   _____

5. What is "stimulated emission"?

   _____

   _____

6. Describe "coherent" and "incoherent light."

   _____

   _____

STEP 4

Examine your notes. Compare your notes for this part of the lecture and your answers to the questions with a classmate. Then look at the sample notes provided in Appendix C (pp. 149–50). Comment on:

- organization
- overall completeness
- use of abbreviations
- clarity of drawings

Are you missing any important information in your notes? Are your definitions and answers to the questions in Step 3 clear and complete? If you are missing important information or have inaccurate information in your notes, you should adopt extra compensating strategies for every lecture you listen to until you are sure you have an accurate understanding of the material. Review the after-class strategies on page 9 again for ideas on how to compensate for what you have missed.

STEP 5

Now let's take a closer look at some of the micro elements (in this first half of the lecture) and the language Professor Winful used to frame them. In Table 3 on page 82, you are given the location of some micro elements and the language clues used. Identify which type of micro element is being illustrated (the second column), and indicate how you could—or whether you should—indicate this in your notes (in the fourth column). Then discuss your answers with a partner. A list of the micro elements you will encounter follows:

- overview/background
- process description
- definition
- summary

Table 3: Micro Elements in Professor Winful's Lecture

Lecturer/location of subsection	Micro element	Language clues/headings	How/whether to record it in your notes?
Winful (1:23–1:36)		"And so today I'm going to tell you a little bit about how a laser works, and also some of the principles that govern the control and manipulation of light."	
Winful (5:53–6:14)		"An electron in the innermost orbit is considered to be in its ground state."(1) "The lowest energy level is the ground state."(2)	
Winful (9:03–9:42)		"This process happens spontaneously, so we call this emission of the photon spontaneous emission." "So, spontaneous emission is the light or the radiation that comes out of an atom when an electron drops down spontaneously from one higher level to a lower level."	
Winful (21:56–22:32)		"So what we've seen here is amplification of radiation. OK, so we've covered these words here. We've seen stimulated emission, how it creates photons that are correlated with one another and therefore lead to coherent light. . . ."	

You should now be familiar with some of the signals that speakers give to show the micro-level organization of a lecture.

One additional interesting micro element illustrated in this section of this lecture is **analogy**. An analogy is a comparison between two things. Often a lecturer will try to make a complex idea more understandable by comparing something complex to something familiar. An analogy can begin with the words *it is like* or *this resembles*. You may miss analogies if you think the professor is departing from the main subject and you stop listening. However, if you wait until the end of the analogy, usually you will see a connection to the present topic. Sometimes analogies are not good ones, but often they can be very helpful. The analogy in this lecture occurs as Professor Winful is describing stimulated emission, and he uses an analogy to describe coherency and incoherency in light.

Table 4: Micro Element of Analogy in Professor Winful's Lecture

Lecturer/location of subsection	Micro element	Language clues/headings	How/whether to record it in your notes
Winful (20:16–20:52)	Analogy/ definition	"Now incoherent is like, say if all of you started talking at the same time in different languages and at the top of your voices and someone walks in here and doesn't know what is going on. It's just babble, right? But of course if you all start talking in the same language, saying the same thing, well, someone out there would hear very loud and uh totally coherent output coming from this room. And that's how you create a choir or a symphony, an orchestra. Okay, everyone is playing together."	

TASK 5

Listen to Clip 16 from 20:16 again as you read the analogy in Table 4. What is *coherency* compared to? Would it be helpful for you to understand the meaning of *coherency* (especially later) by including this analogy in your notes? What would you put in your notes to help you remember it later?

_____

_____

_____

TASK 6

<u>STEP 1</u>

Review again the list of macro organization patterns on page 75. After listening to the first half of this lecture, what do you think the primary micro-organization elements are?

_____

_____

_____

<u>STEP 2</u>

For the first half of the lecture the following micro elements are present (as well as several others). List the order in which these appeared by numbering the blanks 1-5. Discuss your answers with a partner.

definition of ground state _____

summary statement _____

intro/background _____

definition by process description (spon. emis) _____

definition by process description (stim. emis) _____

As we saw in the diagram on page 77, individual micro elements such as definitions, examples, or process descriptions can make up the larger picture of the whole lecture. Sometimes, however, micro elements are quite complex. They can be "layered," since some ideas in a lecture have a hierarchical relationship. For example, in an introduction there could be background, definitions, and an extended example. Within a definition, there could be other new terms introduced and a process description.

One way to think about this "layering" for the first part of the laser lecture is shown in Figure 2:

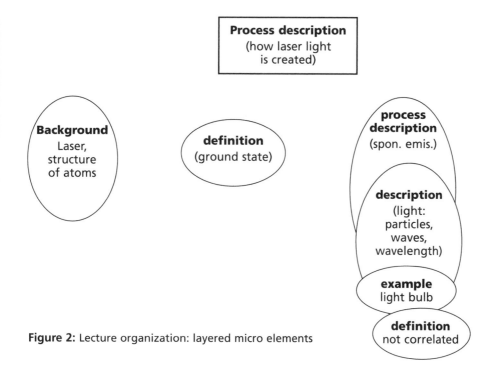

Figure 2: Lecture organization: layered micro elements

This figure is meant to represent the hierarchy of ideas in the process description of spontaneous emission. As Professor Winful describes this process, he also introduces the properties of light, which are necessary to understand at this point, and he gives us an example, the light bulb. He then introduces the term *correlation* by explaining that the photons are not correlated in spontaneous emission.

TASK 7

In the next part of the laser lecture, Professor Winful talks about stimulated emission (15:43 to the end of the first half). Notice the heading here. He begins this portion of the lecture by saying: "Now let's talk about stimulated emission because that's a principle on which the laser works." The micro elements present within this process description are illustrated in Figure 3 on page 86.

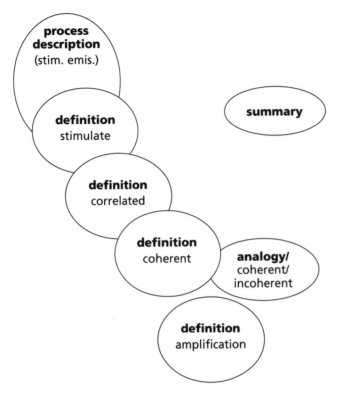

Figure 3: Stimulated emission process: layered micro elements

STEP 1

Did you include all of these elements in your notes? Did you use any method, such as indenting, to show that all of these definitions are part of the process description? With a classmate, discuss how you organized your notes for this part of the lecture.

STEP 2

Discuss how you can best represent hierarchical relationships in your notes. Do you generally practice indenting, or placing the major content area to the left and indenting the subordinate information to the right?

> Recognizing these micro elements will help you to stay focused, recognize what you have missed, and help you to see the bigger picture.

TASK 8 (optional practice)

You have already studied the first half of this lecture (page 80). For extra listening practice, listen to the second half (DVD 2, Clip 17), take notes, and answer the following comprehension questions. If you notice that you cannot answer any of the comprehension questions, you should find a method to compensate for what you missed. If, for example, you notice you couldn't answer Question 1, review your notes, listen to that part of the lecture again, and try to determine why you missed that information. Try to identify which micro elements are present.

Comprehension Questions DVD 2, Clip 17

1. What is "feedback" in a laser? What example does Professor Winful use to describe it?

   _____

   _____

   _____

2. What is "oscillation"? How does Professor Winful define it?

   _____

   _____

   _____

3. What is "pumping"?

   _____

   _____

   _____

4. How do mirrors affect the light in the laser cavity? How does this light come out of the cavity?

   _____

   _____

   _____

5. Why is laser light so directional?

_____

_____

_____

6. What does it mean to "satisfy oscillation conditions"?

_____

_____

_____

7. What does "out of phase" mean? What does "in phase" mean?

_____

_____

_____

8. What are two major applications for laser technology that Professor Winful talks about?

_____

_____

_____

Analysis Questions

TASK 9

1. What strategy did you use when confronted with the many drawings on the board? Did you copy only the drawings in your notes, or did you include some of the commentary?

_____

_____

_____

2. If you had a strong background in physics or electrical engineering, this was probably an easy lecture for you. You can see the importance of background when approaching a lecture and the effect background has on your comprehension. If you did not have a strong background in these subjects and missed some concepts, what strategies did you use to compensate?

_____

_____

_____

3. You may have also noticed in this lecture how Professor Winful builds on each concept he presents. If you missed the definition of *coherency,* for example, early in the lecture, you might have trouble later in the lecture. In addition, you may become fatigued toward the end of a lecture. These factors may cause a kind of compounding of comprehension difficulties toward the latter half of any lecture. What strategies could you use to be sure your comprehension at the end of the lecture is solid?

_____

_____

_____

Definitions are a kind of micro element that you will encounter very frequently in lectures. We will now take a closer look at how lecturers may introduce new terms and the strategies you can use to prepare for them.

Encountering Definitions

Studying New Vocabulary (before the Lecture)

You may find that new terms in a lecture distract you from continuing to listen to the speaker. When you encounter new words, you may find yourself focusing on them too long; as a result, you may miss important new information while you are trying to figure out the meaning or how to spell the unfamiliar term. There are, however, several strategies that you can use to help reduce the stress you face when encountering new terms. One strategy is to become familiar with as many new terms as possible *before the lecture* by previewing the assigned reading material. This should include becoming familiar with how new words are pronounced by looking them up in the dictionary, by going online to one of the dictionary sites such as *merriamwebster.com,* or by using a hand-held dictionary device. In fact, using several strategies is probably the most effective way to handle new terms, especially at the beginning of a class when many new terms may be introduced.

TASK 10

When you are preparing for lectures, it is not sufficient to merely glance at new words that you may encounter. You will need to really study them. A list of some possible strategies for handling new terms that you encounter in your reading material prior to the lecture follows. Indicate the ones you use with a check. Discuss your strategies with a partner.

_____ Scan the reading material for new terms.

_____ Look for definitions in the text.

_____ Look up the definitions in the glossary.

_____ Look up the definitions in the dictionary or on the Internet (*merriamwebster.com*).

_____ Study the pronunciation guide in the dictionary, on the Internet, or with an electronic dictionary.

_____ Ask a native speaker to pronounce new words for you.

_____ Develop new abbreviations for the new terms.

_____ Practice using the abbreviations.

_____ Review new terms and definitions frequently.

_____ Other: _____.

TASK 11

Evaluate your strategies for preparing for new words. Are you using several of the strategies found on the list? Use two or three of these strategies before your next lecture and evaluate their effectiveness. If you were more prepared for the new terms, was the lecture easier to follow with this kind of preparation? If the lecture was not easier to follow, try some different strategies for preparing for new terms.

Knowing how new terms are pronounced and defined will help you not get stuck on the unfamiliar words. Two other helpful strategies are to:

- keep a small notebook with new terms from your classes with you at all times
- frequently review the terms whenever you have a few minutes

Variability in Introducing New Terms in a Lecture

Lecturers introduce new terms in many different ways. One way to introduce a new term is by using it in context and describing what the term means without giving a formal dictionary-type definition. Below you will see a familiar example where a new term is introduced and then it is followed by a synonym and an explanation. This example occurs in Professor Rosenthal's lecture (Clip 1, 2:14). We have already looked at this portion with regard to redundancy.

> Now, I think the first thing when we talk about basic, other basic American characteristics is to recognize diversity. America is a very diverse and heterogeneous country. Many of you come from countries where the population shares a very common history for many, many hundreds of years. That is not true in the United States. We are a land of immigrants, so our background is very diverse. And that means many of our institutions are diverse. So the first thing I wanna say about the American healthcare system is that it is very diverse. So if you said to me: "Choose one word that captures the essence of the American healthcare system." I would have to say diverse, or another word might be heterogeneous. That's a kind of a nice word to add to your vocabulary. But what it means is, there isn't any one system or any one characteristic that describes this whole healthcare system. So the first thing we wanna remember is that it's very diverse in its characteristics.

You can see that she explains the meaning of *diverse* both by using a synonym, *heterogeneous*, and by giving an explanation. If you got stuck on the word *heterogeneous*, and did not continue listening because you were trying to translate, or because you were trying to figure out how to spell it, you probably missed the subsequent explanation.

To listen for clues to the meaning of new terms that may be given in context, it's necessary to adopt a broad approach to your listening so that you begin to follow when speakers give clues to the meaning of new words. Another way a lecturer may introduce a term is by giving an example or by describing a process. A lecturer may use word(s) and then give the explanation, or a lecturer may give the explanation first, followed by the term/word(s). Here is an example of the second type from a dental lecture:

"In this case the patient has no teeth at all, and the technical term for that is *edentulism.*"

When a speaker gives a definition before the new term, you may have difficulties because as a listener, you may not recognize that a new term is being defined until after you have heard the term itself. If the definition has been already given, you have missed your opportunity to write it down.

A lecturer may also define a concept by listing its properties as we saw in Lines 19–22 in the BIO 152 example of what it means to be alive (p. 30).

The next few tasks will ask you to listen to some definitions to help you become more familiar with some common definition forms. Identifying their forms will help you recognize definitions more easily. Here are some common ones:

1. straight forward: term + definition
2. reverse order: definition + term
3. used in context/paraphrase
4. listing properties
5. common term then technical term
6. process description
7. example
8. analogy
9. shown on visual aid (slide, handout)
10. combination of several of the above
11. no definition given

TASK 12

With a partner review the following definitions of *ground state* and *spontaneous emission* from Part 1 of Professor Winful's lecture (DVD 2, Clip 16).

1. Which of the forms from the list do these definitions have?
2. Can you find any redundancy?
3. Can you find the analogy?

Term	Definition
ground state (5:54)	An electron in the innermost orbit is considered to be in its ground state.
	The lowest energy level is the ground state.
spontaneous emission (8:16)	"That process where an electron drops down to the ground state . . . can happen spontaneously. I don't need to do anything to the electron. It just falls. Just like the piece of chalk just fell, without me pushing it. Okay. When it drops to the ground state, it emits light. It emits a photon. Okay. A photon is a particle of light. And so the electron drops to the ground state, and it emits a photon. This process happens simultaneously, so we call this emission of the photon spontaneous emission. So, *spontaneous emission* is the light or the radiation that comes out of an atom when an electron drops down spontaneously from one higher level to a lower level."

_____

_____

_____

_____

TASK 13

For more practice with definitions and their forms, listen to a talk by Professor Keith Alpine, a Professor of Clinical Dentistry at the University of Michigan's School of Dentistry. The lecture is titled "An Overview of the Dental Specialty of Prosthodontics." Prosthodontics is a specialty in the field of dentistry that deals with creating and inserting permanent, artificial teeth into a person's mouth after the person has lost the original teeth due to injury, surgical removal because of tumors, or severe decay. One term to know before you hear the lecture is *osseointegration*. This is the process by which a metal screw, implanted in the bone of the patient, becomes part of the bone.

STEP 1

A list of the new terms you will encounter follows. Create an abbreviation for each term to make your note taking easier. Some sample abbreviations have been given. These terms will be defined for you in the lecture.

Term	Definition
prosthodontics	P
maxillofacial prosthodontics	MP
excised	
prosthesis	
maxilla	
mandible	
edentulism	
partially dentate	
partially edentate	
dentures	
adaptive capacity	

STEP 2

Listen to the lecture two times, DVD 2, Clip 18, and write the key words of the definitions you hear next to the terms on the previous list. If there are any definitions you were unable to understand the first time, listen a second time. Check the accuracy of your definitions with a classmate.

STEP 3

Listen again to Clip 18, and focus on the definitions listed in Table 5. Read the table as you listen a third time.

Table 5: Dental Definitions

Term	Definition	Form
prosthodontics (49:40)	"*Prosthodontics* is that specialty of dentristry that deals with the replacement of missing teeth and their surrounding and supporting structures, both hard and soft tissues, so that's bone, gums, and all these surrounding tissues that have been lost along with teeth."	straightforward: term + definition
maxillofacial prosthodontics (50:00) excised prosthesis	"In some cases the loss of tissues is greater than would normally be the case where a tooth is extracted. This is an example of a patient who has had a tumor *excised* or surgically removed from this area here. And my job is to make a *prosthesis* or an appliance to replace all of the missing tissue in this area. This subspecialty of prosthodontics is known as *maxillofacial prosthodonitics*."	reverse order definition paraphrase for *excised* (or) paraphrase for *prosthesis* (or) term
maxilla mandible (50:59)	"We have two jaws, an upper jaw and a lower jaw. The technical term is for the upper jaw, the *maxilla,* and for the lower jaw, the *mandible*."	common term followed by technical term
edentulism edentulous maxilla (51:17)	"In this case the patient has no teeth at all, and Technical term for that is *edentulism.* So we refer to this upper jaw or maxilla as being an *edentulous maxilla*."	reverse order common term then technical term
partially dentate partially edentate partial edentulism (51:40)	"Some patients have lost a limited number of teeth, as is the case in this patient here, so we would refer to this upper jaw or maxilla as being *partially dentate*. That means that the patient has some of their teeth remaining. But we could also use the term *partially edentate* or we could say that this slide shows *partial edentulism.* In other words there are gaps in the patient's dentition."	reverse order repetition repetition
dentures (52:26)	"Up until recently, when a patient had lost all of their teeth and was rendered edentulous, the patient had only two options available to them. The first was to go without any teeth at all and the second was to wear *dentures.* And that's what this slide shows, an upper complete denture and a lower complete denture."	used in context shown on slide

Table 5: Dental Definitions (continued)

Term	Definition	Form
adaptive capacity (53:32)	"And whether or not a patient is going to be able to wear a lower denture is a function of the individual's *adaptive capacity*. In other words, how well can the individual hold the lower denture in by means of the lips, the cheeks, and the tongue. If the patient is able to master those skills and learn how to hold the denture in, in other words if the patient has a high level of *adaptive capacity*, the success of the lower denture will be high."	used in context (*in other words*)

STEP 4

Lecturers do not purposely give different kinds of definitions to challenge you. They are simply trying to make their lectures more interesting, and they may not be aware that different forms may result in difficulty for students. Professor Alpine, for example, comments on the slides as he gives the definitions. The variation in definition forms provides for a more interesting lecture than a list of textbook definitions.

STEP 5

Focus on the reverse order definitions—for example, the definition of maxillo-facial prosthodontics. What did you do when you originally heard this term? Can you think of a good strategy for trying to write this kind of definition (reverse order) in the real-time constraints of a lecture? For example, in the context of a real lecture situation, you will certainly miss some important definitions. When you miss a definition, you could write a star in the margin of your notes or a question mark to indicate that you need to get that information later.

Because definitions occur frequently in lectures, you will need to continue to practice strategies for preparing for new terms before lectures, recognizing patterns as terms are introduced, and compensating for what remains unclear. Sometimes you may notice that a term the professor introduces is also defined in the text. Even if you know you can go back to the text to get the definition later, try to write the definition the professor gives for practice and then compare it to a classmate's notes or compare it to the text definition. Your professor may even give a definition that differs from the text, so it is always good to listen closely.

Process Descriptions

Process descriptions are another common micro element in lectures. It is important to understand all of the steps in a process and how they are connected to fully understand the process itself. Thus far in our lecture examples, we have encountered process descriptions in several lectures. For example, in Professor Winful's lecture we saw the process descriptions of spontaneous emission and stimulated emission. We also heard at least two process descriptions in Carvajal's lecture: the process description of how zebra mussels kill off other species and the process descriptions of the different methods of coffee production.

Now we will look more closely at the process description from the dental lecture (Clip 18). In the process of inserting a tooth implant, there are definite steps and a definite order to the process.

TASK 14

STEP 1

Listen again to this part (55:05–1:01:42), and review your notes. Professor Alpine begins by saying, "And the first step in the procedure is a surgical step whereby the patient's jaw is operated on under local anesthetic." See if you can identify at least ten steps to this process.

STEP 2

With a partner, use your notes from Dr. Alpine's talk to number these statements in the order that they were presented in the lecture. The first one has been numbered for you.

_____ Once the hole has been drilled, the implant or the fixture is placed into the hole.

_____ And the situation is left for approximately 3–5 months. During this time osseo integration takes place.

___1___ The first step is in the procedure is surgical step . . . and a flap of gum tissues is raised.

_____ The gum tissue is then closed over the fixture.

_____ The next step involves taking a mold or an impression of the mouth over the fixture.

_____ Once the 5- or 6-month period has passed, you can then open up the gum over the fixtures.

_____ This upper part is known as an abutment, and this is attached into the lower screw at the next stage.

_____ From that impression a model is poured up . . . and a crown is fabricated to replace the single missing tooth onto the implant.

_____ The next step involves cutting a hole into the patient's jawbone with precision drills.

_____ To verify osseo integration to make sure that the fixtures have actually integrated into the bone without any sites of infection around them, we take an X-ray.

TASK 15

You may have noticed that Dr. Alpine did not number the steps for you. Instead, he identified the order of the steps in this process description with terms like *first, and then, once…then,* and *next.* You may have had trouble writing the order of the steps, or maybe you had trouble including all of the steps in your notes. Professor Alpine also gave definitions and details throughout this process description that may have made understanding all the steps and their ordering quite challenging. Think about how you can compensate when you miss parts of a process in a real lecture situation. Discuss your ideas with a classmate.

One strategy to help you understand all of the steps in a process is to audio-record the process. You may have discussed in class whether audiotaping or videotaping especially challenging lectures might be useful. Certainly you need to be selective about what you record, and you need to get permission from the instructor to do this. Permission is necessary because lectures are considered to be a kind of intellectual property (at least in the United States and Canada), and taping without consent could make some instructors uncomfortable. Many professors will give their consent when they know you are doing it to understand the material better.

To limit the amount of time you have to spend later listening to the lecture a second time, try this strategy: Turn the recorder on only when you encounter a difficult portion of the lecture. If you have previewed the material to be covered in a lecture, you will be better able to predict which topics will be more challenging.

You have now had a closer look at some important micro elements that occur in lectures. Unit 2 examined background and summaries and how listening to these parts of the lecture can help you make sense of the whole lecture. Unit 3 reinforced these elements and introduced several other elements that can be repeated throughout the lecture. Remember these important micro elements—definitions, process descriptions, extended examples, and analogies.

Next, let's discuss the ways speakers evaluate information.

Qualifying Claims

Earlier we discussed why professors convey information with lectures rather than having students just read the material. One reason we have lectures is so that we can see how experts in the field evaluate issues. Professors evaluate the material they teach and provide a model for knowing how to evaluate the material we encounter. Sometimes a professor will be very direct in his or her opinions. Strong opinions are usually not hard for students to understand. Often, however, professors are more reserved in offering opinions; they make claims that are softened or qualified. We call this softening of a claim **hedging**. A statement that has been hedged has been modified with restricting and limiting words, modals, or weaker verbs. Look at the two statements, one is from the BIO 152 lecture examined in Unit 1:

> **hedged statement:**   My sort of semi-solid definition of life would be...
> **strong statement:**   My definition of life is...

The professor in the BIO 152 lecture used *sort of* and *semi-solid* and the modal *would* to show that he is not yet finished building his definition. He *hedged* to show he was not fully committed to the definition yet.

Academics hedge to show tentativeness and to not overstate things. They prefer to claim only that which data can support. If they make too big of a claim, they leave themselves open for criticism. On the other hand, if they make a narrower, qualified or hedged, claim they are accurately representing ideas, being thoughtful and evaluative, and modeling for students how to be thoughtful and evaluative. Consider the next two statements, the first is from the Rosenthal lecture (Part 4):

> **hedged statement:**   We probably have one of the best healthcare systems
>   in the world.
> **strong statement:**   We have the best healthcare system in the world.

Professor Rosenthal qualifies her claim as you can see by using *probably* and *one of*. She does not make the second (strong) statement, which would be too bold and too broad.

TASK 16

Discuss with a partner the differences in meaning in each of the following pairs of sentences.

1a. **hedged statement**   From an economic perspective you <u>might say</u> that <u>that makes some</u> sense. (Deardorff lecture)

  b. **strong statement**   From an economic perspective that makes sense.

2a. **hedged statement**   In the tropics they <u>tend to</u> plant both corn and beans. (Carvajal lecture)

  b. **strong statement**   Here we always plant only corn together.

3a. **hedged statement**   This change in farming practices has <u>contributed to</u> a loss of biodiversity. (Carvajal lecture)

  b. **strong statement**   This change in farming practices has caused the loss of biodiversity.

TASK 17

Let's examine some of the other hedges from Professor Rosenthal's conclusion to her lecture on the American healthcare system (Part 4). A transcript excerpt is provided (DVD 3, Clip 22 at 22:50). The hedging has been underlined.

Professor Rosenthal's Closing Remarks

Clip 22 at 22:50

1 And we are the most expensive healthcare system in the world, although <u>I think part of</u>

2 the problem is that we're a <u>little more</u> honest with how we gather our statistics than a

3 lot of other countries are so we're <u>probably not as expensive as it seems</u>, if we could get

4 better statistics from other countries.....

Clip 22 at 24:06

5 Okay uh let's just very briefly then talk about the strengths and the weaknesses of the

6 American uh healthcare system and then let's let's listen to your questions.

7 <u>I think uh we can say</u> that <u>we probably</u> have the most advanced and the most pervasive

8 medical technology in in the world, (other countries also do very, very well,) but

9 particularly for a country our size <u>I think</u> we lead the world. And that of course is one

10 reason why we are so expensive.

TASK 18

Listen to the next short segment (DVD 3, Clip 22 at 26:20), and underline the hedging you find on the transcript.

Rosenthal transcript excerpt

Clip 22 at 26:20

11 Okay, so I would argue that one of the strengths in the United States is the medical

12 technology that's available. And I would also argue that we have some of the best

13 care in the world, that doesn't mean you can't get excellent and best care in many

14 other countries, but many people come to the United States, particularly for complex

15 medical problems. Because we we do offer in some of our medical centers what is

16 probably the best healthcare in in the world, <u>I think</u> that has to be acknowledged.

17 And I would also say that we also have weaknesses and I mentioned some of them

18 here and from my point of view and many people's point of view our our most serious

19 weakness is the fact that we do not have equal access to to healthcare for all of its

20 citizens. I, now I express a personal opinion and perhaps also a professional opinion.

21 We are a very wealthy country, and I think we could afford to give health insurance to all of

22 our citizens, but we don't have for some, for a variety of reasons the political

23 will to do that. Perhaps we will accomplish that in the decade to come. I certainly

24 hope so.

In addition to hedging, a speaker (or writer) may sometimes **boost** his or her claim. Boosting can be thought of as the opposite of hedging. Speakers reinforce their claims or make them stronger by citing other researchers and other studies that support their views. Professor Rosenthal boosts her claims in Lines 18 and 20: *and many people's point of view* and *perhaps also a professional opinion.* She indicates that her ideas are supported by many others, and then she states that this is not just her personal opinion but rather her *professional opinion,* meaning an opinion that is supported by many years of study and research.

You can see that she hedges with the word *perhaps* at the same time she boosts! It can indeed be a difficult task to determine the strength of a speaker's claim. Becoming aware of how language is used to indicate a point of view is a first step.

Speakers convey their attitudes and opinions in many ways. They may do so by directly telling us, by repeating information, and also by qualifying or boosting their claims. Professor Rosenthal used all of these methods to indicate her opinions. Now that you are aware of some of the ways speakers convey points of view, listen for them in the next lectures you hear.

TASK 19

Can you think of some good ways to determine if you have correctly understood the professor's claims?

_____

Now you will have a look at some other important things you need to consider when listening to lecture.

Dealing with Visuals

Lecture listening often requires you to do several things at once: pay attention to visual material in the form of charts, diagrams, equations, slides, or text and pay attention to the spoken commentary that accompanies these visuals and write those things in your notes. This difficulty in dealing with the spoken input and the visual input simultaneously is one that all students face. It is a good idea to think about the strategies for addressing this particular challenge to ensure that you understand both the verbal and the visual messages.

Recall the exercise on headings from Professor Swales's lecture on the history of English (pp. 51–53). Professor Swales wrote his details on the board (the visual message); he did not write the headings (the verbal message). The headings were only given verbally. So if you had focused on the visual only—the details—when you reviewed your notes later, you might not have been able to remember the main points. In that lecture (DVD 1, Clips 10 and 11), you needed to record the information given verbally as well as the material written on the board. It is essential to write the main points in your notes, but the details often shown on visuals are also important.

TASK 20

Consider the strategies that you generally use when simultaneously encountering visual and verbal information. Check all of the statements that are true for you.

1. _____ I copy what is presented in the visual as best as I can.

2. _____ I generally ignore the commentary since I am focused on copying the visual.

3. _____ I can generally understand the visuals better than the commentary.

4. _____ I focus on the commentary and plan to get the visual later.

5. _____ I abbreviate everything, copying the Slope of a line on a graph, for example, but not the details.

6. _____ I try to write some commentary.

7. _____ I copy what I can understand in each situation and plan to share notes with a friend later.

8. _____ The slides are available on the Internet/in the book/in the class materials, so I focus on the commentary, knowing that I can go back to the slides later.

9. _____ Other: _____.

TASK 21

STEP 1

Discuss with a classmate if any of these strategies from Task 20 might be better than others. Perhaps some of these strategies may work better in some classes or with certain professors. How can you compensate if you miss the visuals? What can you do if you miss the commentary?

STEP 2

Another important point to consider is whether the commentary is just a description of the visual or if the commentary is *complementary* to the visual. In many cases the commentary is indeed complementary—that is, the commentary includes an evaluation of the visual or an emphasis of a particular point on the visual. If you are focused on copying the visual, you might miss this important evaluation. Which of the above strategies would be good for you to use to make sure you got the main point(s) of the visual(s)?

_____

_____

_____

TASK 22

Discuss with a partner whether you have a regular strategy of determining the accuracy of the visuals and the commentary that you write in your notes.

TASK 23

Review the Carvajal lecture (DVD 1, Clip 12) in which he shows drawings of the methods of coffee cultivation (Clip 12 at 33:47). Review your notes for this part of the lecture. What strategy did you use when listening to this part of the lecture? Did you record the pictures in detail and omit the commentary? How was your strategy affected by the amount of background you had for this part of the lecture (from your Internet search before the lecture)? Discuss your answers with a partner.

Might there be a better strategy for dealing with the visuals in this part of the lecture such as recording a "stick figure" or very simplified picture of the visuals? (Review the sample notes for this lecture in Appendix C on pp. 148–49).

TASK 24

STEP 1

In the dental lecture (DVD 2, Clip 18), did you record any of the images? If so, how did you do it? Do you think you may have missed anything the speaker said while you were recording the pictures?

<u>STEP 2</u>

What can you do to compensate for what you may have missed? Discuss your answers with a classmate.

_____

_____

_____

It is becoming more common for professors to use PowerPoint presentations and to give students their slides as handouts. Sometimes the slides are available on a website for review after class. If you have had a professor who uses PowerPoint, what did you do while you were listening to the lecture? Did you take notes on the handouts? Did you just listen, knowing that you could view the slides later? What kind of compensating is necessary for this kind of lecture? Discuss effective strategies for dealing with PowerPoint lectures.

Recognizing Topic Change

As previously discussed, headings are announcements of topic and subtopics. Sometimes a speaker will clearly indicate when he or she is announcing a new topic or changing the topic, and at other times, the topic change is less obvious. Recognizing some of the less direct signals of topic change is important so that, if the professor fails to signal a topic change overtly with a heading, you do not get lost.

Here are some examples of phrases used to directly state a topic:

- The next aspect I will talk about is . . .
- The (second, third, main) method is . . .
- Now, I'm gonna show you . . .
- Let's get on with. . . .
- There are two more things we're gonna do.
- Ok, yup, alright next thing is . . .

Speakers usually provide several signals when they are about to change a topic, so that even if a clear, direct statement such as _Now I'm gonna talk about X_ is not given, you should be able to recognize some of the other signals. Often signals appear together as a group. You may first hear some kind of conclusion of the previous topic, which may include a summary or an evaluation or emphasis on a particular point. Then there might be a pause as the lecturer goes back to look at notes, and then the speaker may introduce the topic. These three things often signal a topic change. Some common signals follow.

Signals that Could Indicate a Topic Change Is Coming

(especially if several occur together)

Summary or repetition of previous ideas

- *So to conclude then, . . .*
- *So, as I said, . . .*
- *Another way to put it is . . .*
- *So I've talked about X, Y, and Z.*

Emphasis/Evaluative comment

- *The important thing here is . . .*
- *What you don't want to forget . . .*
- *Be careful about . . .*
- *Here's the tricky part now.*
- *This causes some very serious problems.*
- *Some people think that we have too many specialists.*
- *What I'm interested in and hoping for is that China will play a major leadership role.*

Verbal "fillers" in a group

- *Umwellokay*
- *Okaysonow*
- *alrightnow*

Visual cues

- putting up a new visual aid
- erasing the board
- moving to the center of the room
- drinking water

Voice cues

- dropping in voice tone before a new topic (when concluding previous topic)
- rise in pitch
- extra stress
- volume increase
- slower speed
- a longer pause

Commands

- *Have a look at the handout here.*
- *Look at Figure 5 up here.*
- *Notice on the overhead . . .*

Questions

- rhetorical question
- direct question

The signals on this list—if they occur by themselves—do not necessarily indicate that a topic change is occurring. However, when several items occur together, it may indeed indicate a topic change. For example, we have seen that fillers such as *um, okay,* and *alright* may occur at any point in a talk: They can occur between sentences or in the middle of sentences, and fillers alone do not indicate a change in topic. However, fillers strung together like *umnowalright,* followed by a long pause, a rise in pitch and volume, and maybe a change in where the speaker is standing, may indeed signal a topic change. You should begin to listen and watch for **packages** of signals (where several of these elements are present in a group) to help you better identify a change in topic when the speaker does not give a direct, clear heading.

TASK 25

Listen to the first 30 seconds of Professor Winful's lecture, Part 2 (DVD 2, Clip 17), and identify the topic change signals. Check all the signals that you notice on the list, and discuss your list with a partner.

1. _____ evaluative comments about the previous topic

2. _____ voice trailing off at end of previous topic

3. _____ transition statement *(In addition to amplification . . .)*

4. _____ body language signals such as _____

5. _____ longer pause

6. _____ clear, direct statement of topic change

7. _____ a rhetorical question

8. _____ a direct question is asked

9. _____ higher pitch at announcement of next topic

10. _____ slowing of pace of delivery as new topic is announced

11. _____ *okay, alright, um* (string of fillers)

12. _____ new term on the board

TASK 26

For more practice, review Carvajal's lecture (DVD 1, Clip 12). Although Carvajal's lecture style was fairly conversational, there are clear and direct signals of topic change: *Um now, for me, (pause) the thing that I've elected to focus on is coffee* (32:00). This lecture also includes several indicators that a new topic is coming even before that statement. Review this lecture from 29:25 to 32:47, and check the signals that he gives that indicate he is getting ready to move on to a new topic. Listen several times if you need to. Compare your list with a partner.

1. _____ evaluative comments about the previous topic

2. _____ voice trailing off at end of previous topic

3. _____ transition statement

4. _____ body language signals such as _____

5. _____ longer pause

6. _____ announcement of topic coming next

7. _____ a rhetorical question is asked

8. _____ a direct question is asked

9. _____ higher pitch at announcement of next topic

10. _____ slowing of pace as new topic is announced

11. _____ string of fillers

TASK 27

Here are some statements from Ricardo Carvajal's talk. Describe the type of signal each is referring to from pages 106–7.

1. Any practice that covers that much area is gonna have very important ecological consequences.

   _____

2. Um now, for me, what I've elected to focus on is coffee.

   _____

3. What kinds of information did you get?

   _____

4. How many of you drink coffee?

   _____

Notice that the signals of topic change occur in this example in a group. There is an evaluative comment about the previous example, a long pause, an announcement of the topic coming next, and some direct questions. Listening for a set of signals like this will help you identify topic changes within lectures. There are often several clues that a topic change is coming even before a heading is given, and if you can begin to identify these signals, you will have an easier time following a lecture.

Lecturing Style

Today, in many universities, especially in the United States, but also elsewhere, the trend is toward a less formal lecturing style in class. In Unit 1 we explored what Professor Swales has called an "open" style of lecturing, how it has advantages and disadvantages for listeners, and why it might require you to use some alternative strategies for improving your comprehension (p. 22). In Unit 2, we saw how the open style has many features of informality present in everyday speech. Further consideration of some features of formality and informality in speaking style is offered here to help you adjust to different academic listening situations.

Read the following descriptions of formal and informal lectures.

Formal Lecture	Informal Lecture
Lecturer may speak from detailed notes, complete text, or PowerPoint	Lecturer may have few notes, may speak "off the cuff" and very casually
Lecturer is only person talking	Lecturer interacts with audience during lecture, allows interruptions and questions; small-group interactions possible
Lecturer follows obvious organizational pattern	Organization pattern may be difficult to follow
Lecturer uses high degree of formal academic terms, mostly complete sentences	Lecturer may use many idioms, phrasal verbs, and slang

You will probably encounter speakers who are formal in both their lectures and in their interpersonal interactions. Many speakers, however, may not be completely formal or completely informal in their speaking style; rather they will show some features of each style, depending on their personality and the situation. For example, a professor may adopt a more formal style to present new research at an academic conference and a less formal style when lecturing in class. It is also common for professors to have some formal features in their lecturing style and very informal features in their language when they see you in the hallway or during office hours. It is important for you to recognize that speakers shift their styles, and it is important to adjust your listening strategies for different situations.

A formality continuum follows. Imagine that style could be represented on a line with very formal language on the left side and very informal language on the right side.

The level of formality or informality (style) can be demonstrated by a number of features including those language features listed, vocabulary use, the extent to which the class is interactive, and the setting.

Formality Continuum

Formal English	Informal English
• fairly complete and grammatical sentences	• frequent incomplete sentences
• not much slang	• ungrammatical phrases
• fewer fillers	• frequent slang and fillers
• fewer misspeaks	• frequent false starts
• well planned, well organized	

Any speaker's English, not just that of a professor, could be placed on this continuum by evaluating the features of formality and informality present. Speakers generally would be placed nearer to the left if/when they lecture and nearer to the right when they are speaking to you in the hallway after class. Speakers shift their level of formality depending on the situation and context.

TASK 28

Working with a partner, decide where you would put the following speakers on the formality continuum, and give your reasons for that placement.

- Professor Rosenthal (DVD 1, Clip 1)
- the undergraduate in the advising session (DVD 1, Clip 7)
- Professor Carvajal (DVD 1, Clip 12)
- Professor Swales on The History of English (DVD 1, Clips 10 and 11)

TASK 29

Review the strategies listed on page 22 for dealing with open lectures. Discuss with a partner any additional strategies you can suggest for dealing with informal situations.

_____

_____

_____

Giving Advice

Advice is often given during lectures and when meeting in office hours, particularly with regard to what you should focus on in your readings or the assignments. Advice can be given directly or less directly, depending on the speaker, his or her relationship to you, the situation, and the content of the advice. For example, some speakers may tend to be less direct in general; they may favor a softened form of advice and may sound more suggestive or polite. A speaker could also shift directness depending on how strongly he or she feels about the topic. A professor might be very direct at one point, when he or she feels very strongly, and less direct on another point, or he or she could shift from less direct to more direct if he or she realized that a student didn't understand the less direct advice.

Common Forms of Advice

Strong/Overt Forms

<u>My advice is</u> to have that finished by Wednesday in case you have any questions.

<u>I recommend that</u> you read this first.

<u>You should</u> always do the whole set of exercises in case some of them appear on the quiz.

<u>If I were you, I'd</u> focus mainly on the other chapter.

Less Strong/Softened Advice

<u>You might wanna</u> have a look at that chapter we read on....

<u>You wouldn't wanna</u> narrow your options too much.

<u>It might not be in your best interest to</u> take that class next term.

<u>You could/might wanna</u> try the third problem in the set again.

<u>It wouldn't hurt to</u> run over to the library to see if they have it.

<u>If you get a chance try to</u> go back and read the paper on....

<u>Why don't you see if</u> you can find more out about....

TASK 30

Discuss the more softened forms with a partner. Have you encountered these before? Do you recognize them as advice?

> Cultural note: Americans have different styles of interacting—some will be more direct and some will be less direct. Students from some Asian countries may not be used to the stronger forms of advice and may think Americans sound pushy or impolite. Americans generally do not intend to be impolite.

Humor

Often in lectures speakers use humor to connect with their audience, to make a hard subject seem easier, to relax themselves as speakers, or to wake up the audience. However, jokes often contain deep cultural assumptions about shared knowledge that some speakers of English and especially non-native speakers do not have. An additional barrier to understanding is that humor can be sarcastic, where a speaker says the opposite of what is intended but says it with a particular tone—and sometimes with a roll of the eyes—to indicate that he or she meant the opposite of what was spoken. Sometimes a professor may even use what we call **deadpan humor,** which is a method of delivering a joke very smoothly, with almost no intonation variation, and almost no overt indication that a joke has been delivered.

You may remember that in the introduction to the lecture on global AIDS, Professor Pollack made a couple of jokes. In this example, notice the assumptions he made about the background of his audience. You will see an example of deadpan, sarcastic humor.

TASK 31

STEP 1

Listen again one or more times to the Pollack clip (DVD 1, Clip 14, from beginning and for the first minute or so). See if you can understand the joke.

STEP 2

Read the transcript.

Professor Pollack on Global AIDS

1 There was just the world's AIDS conference in Geneva. Did anyone see articles in the

2 newspaper about that? Every two years uh AIDS researchers and prevention people

3 and uh doctors and people involved in AIDS care hold a huge conference on AIDS.

4 Where the plenary session is held in a stadium, some 13,000 people in Geneva,

5 Switzerland each of whom had paid a thousand dollars for the privilege of going and

6 not really being able to hear what the speakers are saying. So that's about what you

7 guys are paying for tuition next year…So uh you may uh find some similarities.

STEP 3

Consider the assumptions he made about his audience. Professor Pollack assumed all of the following about his audience:

- that they know what a plenary session at a conference is
- that they can imagine not hearing a speaker in a huge stadium
- that they know the value of $1,000
- that they know how much tuition costs
- that they will understand the sarcastic link between paying a lot of money and not getting what you paid for

Since some members of his audience laughed, we can say his assumptions about his audience's background were at least partly correct. However, in addition to these assumptions underlying the joke, Professor Pollack delivered the joke without any obvious signal of a joke being told. It was spoken rapidly and in low volume; no visual cue was given, and no verbal signal was given, such as *that reminds me of a funny joke.* Many non-native English speakers in the audience did not laugh, and this is probably why. They did not know a joke was being made.

Maybe now you can understand how difficult jokes can be. Understanding jokes requires language familiarity, a high degree of cultural knowledge, and an understanding of methods of delivery.

Students feel like outsiders when they don't understand the jokes. Some may even feel that they have missed an important point. (In the Pollack example the joke was a very minor point.) Unfortunately, there is no way to immediately give you all of the background knowledge you would need to understand most of the jokes that you will encounter. However, there are a couple of strategies you can use to make yourself more comfortable.

One inventive student offered this strategy for dealing with the jokes that she couldn't understand in lectures: Instead of getting frustrated and feeling like an outsider, she decided to just laugh along with everyone else and enjoy the laughter itself! You could also try to identify where in the lecture the joke took place. write down a key word or two, and ask a classmate about the joke after the lecture.

Another good strategy is to watch or read the news regularly. People often joke about current events or scandals, especially political or financial scandals. If you are familiar with what people are likely to be talking about (you have more background), you are more likely to understand the jokes.

Two additional things to keep in mind are that not every one of the American students is laughing at the jokes either. You can't hear the other people who are not laughing! Sometimes they don't understand it either, and sometimes they may think it was not funny. Finally, don't worry about not understanding the jokes. Jokes are rarely exam material.

TASK 32

Now we will have a look at why some professors tell jokes. Read what the professor from the BIO 152 class had to say about his own sense of humor.

MICASE BIO 152 Lecture Excerpt (not on DVD)

1 Um, okay. Two last things, um number one my sense of humor tends to be a little bit

2 dry um, half the time people don't get that I'm making a joke. Um, I can live with that.

3 Mostly I'm up here amusing myself and and and I like me, so, um that doesn't bother

4 me. Um, uh so if you think I'm, pulling your leg it's possibly true and if you really still

5 are having a question in your head just raise your hand and say: "was that supposed to

6 be a joke?" or something like that. Um.

Here the professor is saying that his students (who are mostly native English speakers) often miss his jokes. He's telling jokes in lecture to humor himself. Notice the phrase: *if you think I'm pulling your leg.* This is an idiomatic expression. Can you guess what it means from the context?

Digressions and Anecdotes

In addition to telling jokes, professors may also tell short stories, or anecdotes, that may or may not be related to the topic of the lecture. If the story is a departure from the stated topic, we call it a **digression.** You may have difficulties with these informal stories in a lecture because you may not immediately see how the story is connected to the lecture and so you might not pay attention. In addition, digressions and anecdotes can be difficult to follow because, like jokes, they may contain references to the culture or current or past media events that you may not know about, rendering the story less meaningful. However, stories may be intended to illustrate a point from the lecture, and you need to try to listen to see if this is the case.

In a digression or anecdote speakers may:

- show the relevance of material covered through an example
- link a topic covered in class or one to be covered to a real-life example
- give an important evaluative critique
- entertain the audience or get the attention of the audience
- kill time (use up the remaining minutes of class instead of starting a new topic)

TASK 33

In the introduction to the lecture on global AIDS, Professor Pollack mentioned the world AIDS conference in Geneva. What do you think his purpose was in mentioning that conference? Do you think that was a digression?

_____

_____

TASK 34

Listen to a MICASE audio clip from the introduction of a radiological health-engineering lecture (DVD 2, Clip 19). This class is concerned with the uses of nuclear energy, the associated health risks that those working with radioactive materials may encounter, and approaches to maintaining the highest level of safety. One topic the class deals with is accident management.

STEP 1

Listen generally to the professor's first comments, and try to identify the topic of the previous class and the topic for that day (from the beginning to about 1:06).

STEP 2

In the next part of the same lecture, notice that the professor digresses significantly from her stated topic. Before you listen, you need some background information. Since the last time the professor met with the class, there were news reports of a plutonium accident in Japan. In addition, the class has a textbook that they call _Cember_. Some of the content here assumes knowledge that we do not share with the class, so don't try to understand all the details. Focus on overall comprehension and strategy issues related to digressions. Read the questions before you listen and try to answer them.

1. How did the professor indicate that she would depart from the stated topic for that day? What intonation and words signaled the departure?

   _____

   _____

2. What does the professor talk about in this digression?

   _____

   _____

3. What is the professor doing in this digression?

_____

_____

_____

_____

4. Do you think it would be important to listen carefully to this digression if you were in this class? Explain.

_____

_____

_____

_____

TASK 35

There are several informal terms and phrases in this digression. They are underlined in the transcript. Listen again and read the transcript. With a classmate, try to determine the meaning of each from the context.

MICASE Radiological Health Engineering Lecture Introduction

1 **Professor:** So everything went okay in my absence despite the fact that we had an

2 overly voberse guest lecturer? Verbose, guest lecturer. silence. Okay homework, went

3 okay?... Holly, <u>what's up</u>?

4 **Student:** Uh, uh this week's homework was a little bit difficult, to finish with the

5 project…

6 **Professor:** Yeah, you do have the project tonight so we're all gonna be, <u>buncha</u>

7 <u>engineers</u> in here talking about ethics from six to eight so this should be, a lotta fun.

8 um, yep. Well it's one of those weeks where you have a little extra, remind me which

9 chapter the homework was on.

10 **Student:** Five.

11 **Professor:** Five which is?

12 **Professor:** hadn't looked at it yet. Okay. What? it's interactions of radiation with oh

13 it's interactions okay and we're just we're supposed to start charged particles today

14 right? Yeah okay so I'm still where, I think we need to be, um, we'll see how things go

15 you've got until Thursday on that we'll try to, cover the charged particles today.

16 mm, we did charged particles already did we not? Didn't we?

17 **Student:** We did yeah.

18 **Professor:** Did we do all of it? The site has lost my bookmark.

19 **Student:** Yeah we did that yeah. We did almost all of it.

20 **Professor:** We did what?

21 **Student:** We did all of it.

22 **Professor:** We did all of it. I think we did because that's what I've got marked down

23 here, okay. We'll do photons today. <u>woo hoo hooray</u>. So you've actually should be

24 able to do the homework we did the charged particles before. Oh before we start um,

25 you happen to have had all the accident management you could possibly want the day

26 of the criticality accident in Japan. Were there any questions about, um, the plutonium

27 accident discussions, uh things you've seen that you didn't uh, understand or that were

28 puzzling to you from a health physics standpoint, or from a nuclear engineering

29 standpoint?

30 **Student:** Have they determined the cause?

31 **Professor:** Yes.

32 **Student:** I mean besides operator error. I mean how, how you can possibly put in six

33 or eight times too much uranium? I mean.

34 **Professor:** It's clear to me they had no engineering controls in the first place, so there

35 were no engineering controls, and some kind of operator error. Why you put,

36 effectively a moderator blanket around a tank where you're doing precipitation of

37 enriched fuels, totally eludes me. Um, I've been following, the Radsafe which is a

38 <u>bunch of junk</u>, and um, also following as being on the board of directors of

39 the, A-N-S <u>there's a lot of e-mail traffic</u> right now about it, and it's no one really

40 knows, but it's sort of, we don't understand it. There was a U.S. accident about this in

41 Idaho, similar to this in Idaho <u>in the sixties or seventies</u>. You've heard that? Yeah,

42 yeah. But um, also a friend of mine is the h- uh s- sp- sp- sp- is in the department of

43 energy and happened to be in California last week on business and was the highest

44 ranking, <u>D-O-E official</u>, on the west coast at the time and <u>she was beeped, on a pager</u>,

45 and told uh can she get on a plane to Japan in the next hour. She's beeped sort of uh,

46 at an odd time. So I expect if she, ended up going over there that uh, she'll tell me

47 <u>what the scoop is</u> but I jus- I think it is just a, simple um, uh, accident, but <u>it comes on</u>

48 <u>the wake of last year</u>, when there was a chemical

49 explosion in a fuel processing plant in Japan. This though has obvious, reactivity

50 implications. Now I looked into Cember and there is a chapter on criticality safety,

40 that um, we may or may not get to, this term I have a feeling we won't get to it this

51 term. At any rate, in that chapter you'll look and there's a certain concentration, of U-

52 two-thirty-five, in, aqueous solution, if you stay below that concentration and have no

53 reflector, you cannot have a criticality accident. This was about twenty times that, it

54 was also a precipitation tank so they're dumping stuff in, and stuff's precipitating, at

55 the bottom. The most difficult part of the computation is to try to figure out, you're

56 gonna try to get doses to try to figure out, the, um the total, energy, and the

57 completeness, of the fission process. This is not gonna work like a bomb because it

58 wouldn't have reached criticality fast enough, and as soon as you start getting it

59 happen in the aqueous solution the geometry, is gonna change. So I suspect, that they

60 poured this stuff in, it started settling, um, and, reached a critical mass because it's

61 twenty times the concentration that's safe, and then had criticality with a large rela- or

62 large release of energy, which then would've blown up and made the hole in the roof.

63 What could then have continued to happen in my opinion is if you s- didn't blow

64 everything, that way you could still have other masses of U-two-thirty-five, forming

65 additional criticalities so you might have had, <u>second hiccups</u> sort of like t- tremors,

66 after- aftershocks after an earthquake.

Source: R. C. Simpson, S. L. Briggs, J. Ovens, and J. M. Swales. *The Michigan Corpus of Academic Spoken English.* Ann Arbor: The Regents of the University of Michigan, 1999.

TASK 36

Note the evaluation that takes place (Lines 34–37): "It's clear to me that they had no engineering controls in the first place, so there were no engineering controls, and some kind of operator error. Why you put, effectively a moderator blanket around a tank where you're doing precipitation of enriched fuels, totally eludes me." We can probably identify the criticism that no engineering controls were in place. The phrase "why X does Y totally eludes me" means "how they could be so careless as to let this happen is beyond my understanding." Notice also the intonation that accompanies *totally*. It is quite strong, indicating a sharp critique.

After this point in the lecture the professor goes on to critique the press coverage of the incident: how the various people in charge responded to the press and the need to be careful when responding to the press in these situations. She does not return to the stated topic for many more minutes.

Not all digressions that you encounter will be this connected to the course content as you may have already experienced. Try to remember though, that what appears to be just talking may in fact be important, relevant material linking the course to the real world.

Signals Inviting Interaction

The example from BIO 152 was a very interactive lecture style where the professor constructed his definition as the students gave their input. This interactive style is common, especially in the beginning of a lecture. Lecturers may begin with a joke or two; some discussion of what was covered previously; and perhaps also an invitation for students to make comments, ask questions, or respond to the lecturer's questions. Some students are often too shy to ask questions or respond in front of a group and often refrain from participating in this portion of the class. You probably noticed that the professor in the BIO 152 example did make a few jokes about the students' answers. The thought of offering an answer that becomes the topic of a joke might scare a student away from participating. In the BIO 152 lecture, the professor was only trying to enliven the interaction and make students think.

Remember also that the professor did not expect complete, grammatically correct answers. He was looking for a few words. One strategy you can use to help you learn how to participate in this kind of interaction is to notice what kind of answers students around you give and how the instructors respond. How do the instructors react in general if a student gives an incomplete or inaccurate answer? Are they harsh and critical, or do they just move on to another student's answer?

Student input allows the instructor to gain important information about the clarity of his or her lecture material and the assignments, as well as serve as an opportunity for students to share what is on their minds. Most instructors care about how students are handling the material and want some feedback from students.

In Carvajal's lecture (DVD 1, Clip 12), the instructor invited interruptions and questions at any time in the lecture. This is common among many professors. Students don't always ask questions during the lecture, but if your professor invites you to do so, you may go ahead and ask questions to clarify what was said.

If you watch Professor Deardorff's lecture (in the Additional Practice Section), notice that at one point a student asks what a tariff is after Professor Deardorff had already defined it. Professor Deardorff did not criticize that student for asking, rather he realized that perhaps he was not entirely clear and invited students to interrupt him if they had other questions.

Some students will opt for interacting with the professor via e-mail or during office hours. Each provides a good opportunity for getting clarification. Remember one cultural assumption in many English-speaking countries is that sometimes a lack of understanding is not the student's fault but the speaker's failure to make things clear.

In Unit 3 you have studied the macro patterns and micro elements commonly used to structure lectures. We have also discussed strategies for handling various other aspects of lectures, such as the simultaneous presentation of visual material and commentary, how topic change may be signaled, some forms of evaluation, and why jokes can be difficult to understand.

Additional Practice Section

This unit has been designed to provide you with more lecture listening opportunities and more opportunities to practice the strategies you have begun to use.

Practice Lecture 1: Professor Rosenthal (Parts 1, 2, 3, and 4)

(DVD 1, Clip 1) (DVD 3, Clips 20, 21, 22)

Strategies you will practice:
- preparing
- identifying missed information and compensating
- noticing emphasis/redundancy
- noting style/organization
- practicing accuracy recording numbers
- understanding a speaker's purpose
- looking at the whole lecture to determine a speaker's purpose

TASK 1

Rosenthal Part 1 (DVD 1, Clip 1)

You have already studied this portion of the lecture in the diagnostic that you completed (Unit 1). Here are two questions for discussion:

1. Discuss Rosenthal's points about choice and individualism. To what extent are these values present in the healthcare systems in other countries that you are familiar with?

2. To what extent do you see these values reflected in other aspects of life in the United States?

TASK 2

Rosenthal, Part 2 (DVD 3, Clip 20)

STEP 1

Discuss with a partner what you already know about the training of medical doctors. How many years do they study to become a general practitioner? How many years to become a specialist?

STEP 2

Listen to the second segment of the Rosenthal lecture (DVD 3, Clip 20). Take notes in the space below. You will need to answer questions from your notes.

_____

_____

_____

_____

_____

_____

STEP 3

Answer the Questions: Organization

1. How does Professor Rosenthal signal that she is starting a new topic?
    (Include the words she uses as well as body movements.)

    _____

    _____

    _____

Answer the Questions: Detail

2. How many doctors were there in the United States in the 1990s?

    _____

3. How many medical schools were there at the time of Professor Rosenthal's
    lecture (in 1998)?

    _____

Answer the Questions: Evaluative Comments

4. What adjectives does Professor Rosenthal use to describe the training of
    medical doctors?

    _____

    _____

    _____

Answer the Questions: Detail

5. How does this training period contrast with training in other countries?

    _____

    _____

6. Outline the process of becoming a specialist in the United States.

    _____

    _____

    _____

    _____

7. What percentage of doctors becomes specialists in the United States?

8. Describe the debate surrounding specialists that Professor Rosenthal mentions.

STEP 4

Identify What You Missed and Compensate

1. Compare your notes with your partner and fill in any gaps that you can find.

2. If you missed more than one of the comprehension questions, listen to the same lecture segment a second time.

3. Add any information you missed the first time, and check again to determine why you missed that information.

STEP 5

Discussion Question

1. What do you think about the percentage of specialists in the United States? How is this both an advantage and a problem?

_____

_____

TASK 3

Rosenthal, Part 3 (DVD 3, Clip 21)

STEP 1

1. What are the two most significant problems regarding healthcare in your native country?

_____

_____

_____

_____

2. What strategies has your government employed to address these problems?

_____

_____

_____

STEP 2

Listen to the third segment of Professor Rosenthal's lecture, (DVD 3, Clip 21). Take notes in the space.

_____

_____

_____

_____

_____

_____

STEP 3

Answer the Questions: Organization

1. How does Professor Rosenthal signal that she is starting a new topic? (Include the words and intonation as well as body movements.)

_____

_____

_____

Answer the Questions: Main Idea

2. What is the first major problem internationally that Professor Rosenthal mentions?

_____

_____

_____

3. Where do most Americans get their healthcare insurance?

_____

_____

_____

Answer the Questions: Detail

4. What are the three groups of people for which the federal government provides healthcare?

_____

_____

_____

Answer the Questions: Main Idea

5. What is Medicare?

_____

_____

_____

6. What is Medicaid?

_____

_____

_____

7. What are "HMOs" and "managed care" plans? How do they control
   costs?

_____

_____

_____

8. What are the two things that are clashing with regard to American values and the American healthcare system?

_____

_____

_____

Answer the Questions: Main idea

9. What is the second major problem that the U.S. healthcare system faces according to Professor Rosenthal?

_____

_____

_____

Answer the Questions: Detail

10. What percentage of Americans received insurance from their employers at the time of this lecture?

_____

_____

_____

11. What percentage of Americans do not have health insurance, and what are some of the reasons?

_____

_____

_____

Answer the Questions: Main Idea

12. What is one overriding health policy issue that the United States and many other countries face?

_____

_____

_____

STEP 4

Identify What You Missed and Compensate

1. Compare your notes with your partner, and fill in any gaps that you can find.

2. If you missed more than one of the comprehension questions, listen to the same lecture segment a second time.

3. Add any information you missed the first time, and check again to determine why you missed that information.

STEP 5

Discussion Questions

1. What are your reactions to the information about unequal access to healthcare in the U.S. that you just heard about?

_____

_____

2. In your opinion, how could costs be controlled while providing access for those who are currently not insured?

_____

_____

TASK 4

Rosenthal, Part 4, Preparation

<u>STEP 1</u>

In the final portion of the lecture (DVD 3, Clip 22), you will practice writing some statistics and you will hear Professor Rosenthal repeat all of the main ideas. *Briefly* review your notes from the previous parts of the lecture to remember the main points.

<u>STEP 2</u>

While listening to this part of the lecture, you will practice listening to and accurately recording numbers. The information Professor Rosenthal wrote on the blackboard at the time of the lecture has been deliberately removed. You should try to take notes on the numbers by listening to the numbers; you will also hear some final statistics relevant to this topic.

Listen to Rosenthal, Part 4, Clip 22. Take notes in the space.

_____

_____

_____

<u>STEP 3</u>

Answer the Questions: Detail

1. How many doctors were there in the United States in 1998?

    _____

2. How many nurses were there?

    _____

3. How many hospitals were there?

    _____

4. How many hospitals were owned by the government?

    _____

5. How much did the United States spend per capita on healthcare in 1991?

    _____

Answer the Questions: Detail

6. What percent of the GDP was this in 1991?

_____

Answer the Questions: Main Idea

7. What are the strengths and weaknesses of U.S. healthcare?

_____

_____

_____

Answer the Questions: Main Idea

8. What are the two things that drive healthcare costs up?

_____

_____

STEP 4

Identify What You Missed and Compensate

If you missed any of these questions, examine your notes and try to identify why. Watch the segment again if you missed more than one question. If you need more practice with numbers, make a note of this. Be sure to double-check the statistics in your notes in the future until you are confident that your accuracy has increased.

STEP 5

Discussion Question

1. What do you think was most interesting and informative about this part of the lecture?

_____

_____

_____

TASK 5

Analysis Questions for An Overview of the American Healthcare System by Professor Marilyn Rosenthal

1. What do you think Professor Rosenthal's overall purpose in this lecture was?

   _____

   _____

   _____

   _____

2. Did you notice any statements that Professor Rosenthal made later in the lecture that referred back to her first section on American cultural values? (see Rosenthal Clip 22)

   _____

   _____

   _____

   _____

3. Would you have understood the overall purpose of the lecture if you had missed the introduction?

   _____

   _____

   _____

   _____

4. Make a list of the characteristics of this lecture that made it relatively easy to follow.

   _____

   _____

   _____

   _____

5. To what extent you think Professor Rosenthal is a typical speaker? What do other speakers do/not do that might make listening comprehension more problematic? How can you adapt to each of these?

_____

_____

_____

_____

Practice Lecture 2: Professor Deardorff: International Trade Issues and Less-Developed Countries

TASK 6

STEP 1

Think about what you may already know about some international trade issues. What are some of the international trade conflicts that you are aware of? What are hot topics regarding trade in your country?

_____

_____

_____

STEP 2

Discuss with a partner or look up on the Internet these terms: WTO, NGO, farm subsidy.

_____

_____

_____

_____

STEP 3

Professor Alan Deardorff and Professor Robert Stern have written a paper to advise policy makers. You can find a copy of the paper at: *www.personal. umich.edu/~alandear/*

1. Select "My writings."

2. Select the 2003 paper with Robert M. Stern entitled "Enhancing the Benefits . . . "

Skim the first part of the paper to prepare yourself for the lecture. (Skip the numerical portion.)

STEP 4

Listen to Professor Deardorff's lecture (DVD 3, Clip 23). This lecture was recorded in 2004. Take notes on a separate page, and answer the comprehension questions that follow.

1. Professor Deardorff has a lengthy introduction where he says among other things that the international community ought to "tip the international negotiations in favor of the developing nations." What does he mean and what reason does he give for this?

    _____

    _____

    _____

2. What is one main purpose of the WTO? Briefly describe its history.

    _____

    _____

    _____

3. What are two requirements for nations who want to belong to the WTO?

    _____

    _____

    _____

4. Describe what "Most Favored Nation" (MFN) treatment means.

    _____

    _____

    _____

5. What has been the overall result of GATT and the WTO in terms of tariffs?

    _____

    _____

    _____

6. Explain why there have been high tariffs on the export of textiles from developing countries even though these countries belong to the WTO.

    _____

    _____

    _____

7. What is Professor Deardorff's opinion about what developing countries did and about tariffs in general?

    _____

    _____

    _____

8. What were two things that happened during the Seattle meeting that caused it to fail, according to Professor Deardorff?

    _____

    _____

    _____

9. How was this failure a "wake-up call"?

    _____

    _____

    _____

10. What exactly is the Doha Round?

_____

_____

_____

11. What are three examples of NGOs that are mentioned? What do they want?

_____

_____

_____

12. What is Professor Deardorff's prediction about the results of the Cancun Round? Why does this not worry him?

_____

_____

_____

13. Professor Deardorff mentions *monstrous* policies that developed countries have used with regard to agricultural trade. What are two that he mentions?

_____

_____

_____

14. How can depressed food prices on the world market be both good for some and unfortunate for some, according to Professor Deardorff?

_____

_____

_____

15. What is Professor Deardorff's opinion as to whether the EU is likely to reduce farm subsidies, and what does he think is the "only hope" for future subsidies in agriculture?

_____

_____

_____

16. Describe the process of how subsidies to farmers decrease prices on the world market.

_____

_____

_____

17. What are "patents," "copyrights," and "trademarks"?

_____

_____

_____

18. What is Professor Deardorff's opinion about intellectual property rights and their extension into the developing world?

_____

_____

_____

19. What was the "small step" taken at Doha regarding pharmaceutical property rights for drugs to fight AIDS and tuberculosis?

_____

_____

_____

20. What is Professor Deardorff's hope for what China can contribute by joining the WTO?

_____

_____

_____

STEP 5

Answer the analysis questions.

1. We were not given a roadmap introduction, though Professor Deardorff did provide some hints about his intentions in this lecture. Listen again from the beginning and for the first five minutes, and notice how he indicates his intentions.

2. Here is a segment of transcript where Professor Deardorff offers part of his opinion about intellectual property rights. Is he hedging anywhere? Underline any hedging you can find.

Professor Deardorff Transcript Excerpt

1 Although we need to have these intellectual property laws, we should not extend them

2 to everyone in the world. And so I'm much more skeptical about this stuff than a lot of

3 people are . . .

4 There is nothing in economics, in economic theory that says that intellectual property

5 rights ought to exist or certainly to be extended to everybody. Uh there is nothing in

6 economic theory to do that . . . and so it seemed to me that the optimal thing to do with

7 intellectual property rights would be to have them in countries that can afford

8 them, the rich countries. Uh, but not so much in the countries that cannot.

---

3. What do you think his overall purpose for this lecture was?

_____

_____

4. Professor Deardorff spoke fairly rapidly and without much visual support. What strategies did you use to follow his lecture, (e.g., before lecture, during lecture, and after the lecture)?

_____

_____

_____

_____

APPENDIX A

Useful Abbreviations and Symbols for Note Taking

One of the difficult aspects of taking notes in a second language is that you need to have a system of abbreviations developed and you need to abbreviate and use symbols to increase the completeness and clarity of your notes. The following is a list of some commonly used abbreviations and symbols that you should try to use, or you may develop your own. You will certainly need to develop abbreviations for the significant content terms in your classes. Please refer to the sample notes for ideas on how to abbreviate content terms in the lecture included in this text.

Useful Abbreviations and Symbols for Note Taking

Term	Abbreviation or Symbol	Term	Abbreviation or Symbol
amount	amt.	increase	↑
approximately	~	large	lg.
and	&, +	less than	<
at	@	maximum	max.
because	bec.	minimum	min.
cause	→	percent	%
decrease	↓	population	pop.
different from	≠	point	pt.
dollars	$	regarding	re
not equal to	≠	small	sm
equal to	=	thousand	K
for example	i.e.	with regard to	w/r/t
greater than	>	within	w/in
important	imp.	without	w/o

TASK 1

For the next lecture you listen to, think about some key terms you will encounter and make a list of abbreviations for those terms. Try to use these abbreviations in your notes. Compare your notes with a classmate.

APPENDIX B

Lecture Comprehension Evaluation Form

Student:_____

1. _____ can identify most/some/a few major topics.
2. _____ can identify most/some/a few supporting ideas and examples.
3. _____ can show how most/some/a few supporting ideas relate to major topics.
4. _____ can recognize most/some/a few key definitions.
5. _____ can guess most/some/a few word meanings from context.
6. _____ can identify most/some/a few evaluative comments.
7. _____ can record visuals clearly/partially and most/some/a little verbal commentary.
8. _____ records numbers accurately usually/sometimes/rarely.
9. _____ uses a wide variety of/some/a few preparation/compensation strategies.
10. _____ is listening broadly/narrowly.

Areas of progress:

_____

_____

_____

_____

Suggestions for improvement:

_____

_____

_____

_____

APPENDIX C

Sample Notes

Notes for Rosenthal Lecture

Overview of US Healthcare Syst

Few words about America
3 Character. Reflected in ↑

    1. cult. hist /values ⎫
    2. polit. syst.   ⎬ true for any social inst. incl relig, fam, educ.
    3. econ philos ⎭

1. Diverse *** imp. feature - heterogeneous
    No 1 charact. describes it

2. Individualism
    choice v. imp.

3. Market-oriented
    part of capitalist dynamic

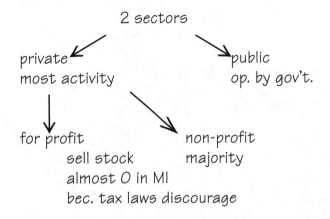

2 sectors

private
most activity

public
op. by gov't.

for profit
    sell stock
    almost 0 in MI
    bec. tax laws discourage

non-profit
majority

healthcare syst more than hosp.
largest grp:
pharmaceuticals
1000s small co. on cutting edge research - exciting
    medical equip. data services

Research
Am leads wld in amount
more $ givn
biggest source-fed gov't (NIH)

also private foundations

Notes for BIO 152 Definition

What's Alive?
Bio- study of life
    Alive?   Properties
                 react - resp to env.
                 reproduce (capability)
                 consume energy
                 cells
                 growth - size and #
                 evolution-adaptation
semisolid def.
    Can convert mtls from envir. into copies

Cloning is reprod? Yes asexual
Virus? No - no metab.
Apple seeds? - dormant but capable -Yes alive
Coma? Metab, but no response

Notes for Swales Lecture on a Brief History of English

E is not old
3 periods
700-1100   old E. Anglo Saxon nobody knows
1100-1500   Middle E. German+French
1500-Modern E

1066 North France invaded Engl.   Norman Conquest

E. Never pure, always a mix

<u>German</u>   <u>French</u>
cow, swine   beef, pork
sheep, deer   mutton, venison

Why the diference?
Lower class raising animals   upper class, eating it

1600 Shakesphere Rennaisance added Latin + Greek
      Chemistry, Phys, Astron. Use L + G
      Latest discipline: Comp Sci. 1950s terms from everyday life
         (to boot up)
      Nobody study L + G

Rise of E. v. recent and v. rapid
      E. was minor L for many cent.
      1800 imp. W/ expan of U.S.
      1900 really imp.

E. major L of internat'l research - not always like that

Schol. L ↑ and ↓ dep. on new info.
If no new info publish → no point of learning it

1st schol L   Sanskrit (4-5000 yrs ago)
                Chinese
                Ancient Greek
                Arabic
                Rennais. Latin
                German 19th cent., mod. L
                English
Interest. Q   Will E. be replaced? Spanish? Chinese?

Notes for First Part of Carvajal Lecture

Overview of Agroecology
Ecology what is it?
   <u>Not</u> spiritual movem. - activism (misconception)
   "the scientific study of factors that determine distrib. & abund. of
      organisms"
     distribution - where things loc. in space
      pine trees why here, not there?
        <u>Ex. in MI</u>
         How complicated can get
          <u>Zebra mussel</u> has stripes
          15 yrs ago none in N. Am
          1988 1st arrive in L. St. Clair → now all over
          central US - econ/environ. <u>disaster</u>
          mussels stick to anything hard, pipes - clog - shut
          plants down - power/nuclear pipes, killed off nature -
          other clams, fish

How 1 org. create so many problems?
(Q Agroecologists ask)
   Q What does it eat? (algae)
   Q How reproduce? (spawn v. freq.)
   Q How many need to put in lake to have pop. explode?

Org. → population → community

Q What is relationship betw. this and other species?

Ex. of how reproduce: sq m = 1 mil. Mussels: kill off natives

↑ zebra mussel → compete for food - none left for small fish =
↓ plankton,
↓ (big fish, ↓ fishermen, ↓ food)

How get here?
commercial ships in Europe - cargo + H2O then H2O dumped into
waterways at arrival in US + zebra mus.

Consequence
<u>Loss of biodiversity - # of species ↓</u>
significant: we don't underst. what all species do bef. extinct
has lot peop. worried

Agroecology
Ec. of agricultural systems

Notes for First Part of Winful Lecture

What's a Laser?
Herbert Winful - Prof. EECS - optics res.   "study of light"
                                            how travels, how use, principles
                                               that govern

Light—skip for now
Amplification
Stimulated
Emission of
Radiation

Amplification - where light comes from

   Atom - dense nuc., protons   "not real accurate pict."
       neutrons, elect. (may spin around)

each orbit has dif. energy level

_____ upper   higher state = higher energy
_____
_____
_____ ground - (inner orbit) = **ground state** = lowest energy = stable

   promotion methods → light, heat, elect. pulse

—⊖—^{e}— 〰〰➤ photon   { e is not in stable st.
   ↓   ground   wants to drop down
_____   can happen spontaneously

   ↓

spontaneous emission

   back to LIGHT - photon has color
                  - a stream of particles (photons)
                  - can act as a wave 〰〰➤   <u>ocillates</u>

   color of light related to sep. energy levels λ = wave length
   ex. laser red light 620 nm ⟍
                         680 nm ⟩ range determines color nm = 10^{-9} v. short
                                     (1/billion)
   when e drops - range of λ assoc w/e
   a range of colors result

spontaneous emission - photons come out - diff. directions
                                              diff
                                              diff properties
                                              = incoherent = not correlated
                                                 w/each other

stimulated emission

   —⊖—^{e}—   —⊖—^{e}—   —⊖—^{e}—   —⊖—^{e}—
    ↓ 〰➤   ↓ 〰➤   ↓ 〰➤   ↓ 〰➤
   ____ photons   ____ 〰➤   ____ 〰➤   ____ 〰➤
                                     〰➤   〰➤
                                                     〰➤

   e can stimulate another atom - both photons trigger/stim. another etc.
   = identical photons
   = photons are correlated in stim emis

Bibliography

Benson, M. "Lecture Listening in an Ethnographic Perspective." In *Academic Listening: Research Perspectives,* edited by J. Flowerdew. New York: Cambridge University Press, 1994.

Chan, Y. P. "Language in Lecturing: A Study of Discourse Markers in Computer Science and Information Systems Lectures." Master's thesis, City University of Hong Kong, 1995.

Chaudron, C. "Academic Listening." In *A Guide for the Teaching of Second Language Listening*, edited by D. Mendelssohn and J. Rubin. San Diego, CA: Dominie Press, 1995.

Chaudron, C., and J. Richards. "The Effect of Discourse Markers on the Comprehension of Lectures." *Applied Linguistics* 7 (1986): 113–27.

Dudley-Evans, T. "Variations in the Discourse Patterns Favored by Different Disciplines and Their Pedagogical Implications." In *Academic Listening: Research Perspectives*, edited by J. Flowerdew. New York: Cambridge University Press, 1994.

Dyer, J. "The Professorial Anecdote: An Invisible Genre." TESOL presentation. Orlando, FL. 1997.

Flowerdew, J., ed. *Academic Listening: Research Perspectives*. New York: Cambridge University Press, 1994.

——— "Definitions in Science Lectures." *Applied Linguistics* 13 (1992): 202–19.

——— "Research Relevant to Second Language Lecture Comprehension—An Overview." In *Academic Listening: Research Perspectives*, edited by J. Flowerdew. New York: Cambridge University Press, 1994.

Flowerdew, J., and L. Miller. "The Teaching of Academic Listening Comprehension and the Question of Authenticity." *English for Specific Purposes* 16 (1997): 27–46.

Jones, J. F. "From Silence to Talk: Cross-Cultural Ideas of Students' Participation in Academic Group Discussion." *English for Specific Purposes* 18 (1999): 243–59.

Lynch, T. "Promoting EAP Learner Autonomy in a Second Language University Context." In *Research Perspectives on English for Academic Purposes*, edited by J. Flowerdew and M. Peacock. Cambridge: Cambridge University Press, 2001.

——— "Training Lecturers for International Audiences." In *Academic Listening: Research Perspectives*, edited by J. Flowerdew. New York: Cambridge University Press, 1994.

MacDonald, M., R. Badger, and G. White. "The Real Thing?: Authenticity and Academic Listening." *English for Specific Purposes* 19 (2000): 253–267.

Mason, A. "By Dint of: Student and Lecturer Perceptions of Lecture Comprehension Strategies in First-Term Graduate Study." In *Academic Listening: Research Perspectives*, edited by J. Flowerdew. New York: Cambridge University Press, 1994.

Mendelssohn, D. *Learning to Listen: A Strategy-Based Approach for the Second Language Learner.* San Diego, CA: Dominie Press, 1994.

Mendelssohn, D., and J. Rubin. *A Guide for Teaching Second Language Listening.* San Diego, CA: Dominie Press, 1995.

Murphy, J. "Integrating Listening and Reading Instruction in EAP Programs." *English for Specific Purposes* 15 (1996): 105–20.

Olsen, L. A., and T. N. Huckin. "Point-Driven Understanding in Engineering Lecture Comprehension." *English for Specific Purposes* 9 (1990): 33–48.

Oxford, Rebecca L. *Language Learning Strategies: What Every Teacher Should Know.* New York: Newbury House/Harper & Row, 1990.

Pickering, L. "The Structure and Function of Intonational Paragraphs in Native and Nonnative Speaker Instructional Discourse." *English for Specific Purposes* 23 (2003): 19–43.

Rost, M. "On-line Summaries as Representations of Lecture Understanding." In *Academic Listening: Research Perspectives*, edited by J. Flowerdew. New York: Cambridge University Press, 1994.

Swales, J. *Research Genres: Explorations and Applications.* New York: Cambridge University Press, 2004.

Tauroza, S. "Second Language Lecture Comprehension Research in Naturalistic Controlled Conditions." In *Research Perspectives on English for Academic Purposes*, edited by J. Flowerdew, and M. Peacock. Cambridge: Cambridge University Press, 2001.

Tauroza, S., and D. Allison. Expectation-Driven Understanding in Information Systems Lecture Comprehension." In *Academic Listening: Research Perspectives*, edited by J. Flowerdew. New York: Cambridge University Press, 1994.

Thompson, S. "Frameworks and Contexts: A Genre-Based Approach to Analyzing Lecture Introductions." *English for Specific Purposes* 13, no. 2 (1994): 171–86.

Varttala, T. "Hedging in Scientifically Oriented Discourse: Exploring Variation According to Discipline and Intended Audience." Doctoral dissertation, University of Tampere, Finland, 2001

Young, L. "University Lectures—Macro Structure and Micro Features." In *Academic Listening: Research Perspectives*, edited by J. Flowerdew. New York: Cambridge University Press, 1994.

Notes

Notes